ROYAL TOY SPANIELS

ALICIA PENNINGTON

RINGPRESS

Acknowledgements

I should like to acknowledge the help and assistance given by Barbara and William Burrows of Thos. Fall. They spent many hours researching and reproducing old photographs and their beautiful reproductions speak for themselves. David Barker also spent a day taking photographic shots for which we are very grateful.

Jaki Canning is the artist responsible for the excellent drawings. I am most appreciative of her skill and understanding. The task of typing the manuscript from my scrawling writing fell to an ever-patient friend Mrs Jean Smith, who coped with all her family, both human and animal, and still came up with the copy on time.

Throughout the years, my husband George and daughter Julia have helped, supported, and criticised when necessary. This book is a way of saying thank-you for the past, present and future.

Finally, to all the friends and breeders who have supplied material and photographs and above all for their friendship through the years – thank-you. Particularly, Tom O'Neal and Ron Fabis who supplied photographs and material from America. Kurt Ogevall whose charming history of the Swedish King Charles took him many evenings of work and research. Sylvie Desserne from France who sent details of both King Charles and Cavaliers. Virginia Barwell of the Charlottetown Cavaliers for her time and her valuable material for the present-day history of the Cavaliers. Jane Bowdler, who, as the Historian for the Cavalier King Charles Spaniel Club, lent me copies of her mother's papers and photographs. There are so many people whose help I shall always remember, including Julia Barnes, who with her editor's knife has striven to get a quart into a pint pot and Mrs Susie Jones for her invaluable help proof reading.

Published by Ringpress Books Limited 1989

Spirella House, Bridge Road, Letchworth, Herts SG6 4ET

© 1989 Alicia Pennington

Printed in Great Britain at The Bath Press, Avon

ISBN 0 948955 708

Contents

Tudorhurst King Spaniels, bred by Alicia Pennington.

Thomas Fall

Introduction

DOGS have been an important part of my life for as long as I care to remember. My earliest recollections are of daily rides with my father accompanied by six Cocker Spaniels, a Labrador, a pair of Cairns (who had rat and snake killing down to a fine art), a Bull Terrier (who blushed) and the occasional couple of Fox-Hound pups. On occasions this motley mob must have looked even more ridiculous when accompanied by my father's pet Himalayan bear. Unfortunately he became a little too inquisitive and playful for his own good and was relegated to our own grounds. I loved those early morning rides in India, relishing the space and the freedom.

On my eighth birthday I received what was to become one of my most treasured possessions – *Dogs in Britain* by C. L. B. Hubbard. The book still falls open at page 254, the King Charles Spaniel: 'The refined sturdiness and intelligent liveliness is hard to find in another dog so small in Britain today.' I remember reading those words as though it was yesterday. The accompanying illustration showed a photograph of Lady Bayard of Braemore by Thomas Fall. I was completely captivated. I knew then that what I wanted most was a King Charles. I pleaded, I demanded, but to no avail. My father was adamant: 'We are not having a breed that looks as if it has run into a brick wall.' I reminded my father that we had a Peke called Ming. 'That's different,' was the illogical reply of my parent.

It was not until George and I married in 1956 that I produced my well-worn book again. I have never discovered if it was still the rosy hue of the honeymoon or just absent-mindedness that occasioned his comment: 'What an attractive little dog.' I did not hesitate. The next day I was at Euston to collect Melanie, a small seven-week-old black and tan with the face of a Pansy, who had travelled up from St Ives, in Cornwall. The message was: 'Twelve guineas and please return the basket.' I paid and I returned the basket. Clutching my little black and tan in her dusky pink pullover I hailed a taxi for St John's Wood. In the taxi I unwisely started to remove the jersey – it was an all-time flea circus! Not being prepared for the event, I had no flea powder or insecticidal shampoo, but I remembered Nanny's old remedy, vinegar. I poured the contents of a vinegar bottle into a large saucepan. There was not enough, so I added the vinegar, pickling spices and pickled onions from George's store. I warmed the whole concoction and poured it over little Melanie. Whether it was the vinegar, onions or pickling spice, the fleas met an early demise, asphyxiated no doubt. I then shampooed Melanie with my shampoo but the onion and vinegar seemed to be winning. I tried to drown the whole stench with Elizabeth Arden Blue Grass. I need not have bothered, as I was informed the whole place smelt like an Eastern brothel!

Melanie had all the charm and wiles of the King Charles. My father was entranced by her and remarked he could never understand why we had never had one of these funny little dogs before. Melanie had ambitions to be a gun dog. She would work a cover with the best of them, but sadly, she had the most shocking hindquarters, which hampered and tired her in her latter years. I vowed then that I would only breed from sound dogs and would do my utmost to eradicate slipping patellas. It all seemed so easy to me then – naive, young and ready to change the world. Melanie was soon joined by Alexandra; I bought her from Crufts to found a dynasty. Poor Alix was an epileptic, so that was that as far as breeding was concerned.

In 1958 I met Mrs Violet Jackson of the Homehurst's, a charming and forthright lady. She expected her King Charles Spaniels to be sound, tough and obedient – and they were! I told this very kind, and not always patient lady, of my dreams for King Charles. I owe so much to her and to Captain Jackson for letting me have Carolyn of Homehurst and her grandchildren Merry Monarch and Merry Maid of Homehurst, and also for all the practical advice they gave me. Through Captain and Mrs Jackson we met Stanley and Pauline Sharp of the Zubaidas. Pauline has all the charm and gentleness the King Charles personifies. She taught us so much about King Charles, their little foibles and the extra care these little Royal Spaniels warrant. Pauline supplied us with Royal Richard of Zubaida and later, on my daughter Julia's tenth birthday, she presented us with Sambo of Zubaida, the foundation of the Curtanas, a beautiful sound black and tan and another frustrated gun dog. In fact, Melanie took Julia and Sambo for tuition. Sambo enjoyed life to the full, he approached everything he did with enthusiasm. On a shoot he was apt to forget his manners and launch himself at any dog he considered was encroaching on his birds. He confused and terrified one poor Labrador so much, that the poor dog decided the only safe place to retrieve from was the gamekeeper's

*Alicia's daughter
Julia with Merry
Monarch.*

wagon, which did little for the reputation of the expensively trained gun dog! When Julia was at boarding school during the week, Sambo was quite well behaved; but on Friday, with Sambo ensconced in the car waiting to collect Julia, all hell would be let loose as we drove up the school drive, and there was no peace until he found Julia. Sunday evenings would find Sambo disconsolately sitting on the suitcase trying his hardest to be packed as well. The return journey to school was always quite dreadful. If you looked in the car mirror you would see a tearful little girl clutching an equally miserable King Charles, who would proceed to sulk for two days. Sambo's granddaughter Morgana inherited many of his characteristics, particularly his great sense of fun.

Over the years we have owned and come into contact with many different breeds, but for us it is the King Charles who have all the charm, intelligence and strength of character. They are all such individual dogs; their sense of fun and devotion to their owners make them the ideal companions. A Swedish friend told me her vet remarked that the King Charles was the dog for the connoisseur, a very charming description. For me, life without a King Charles Spaniel would be unthinkable.

The lifelong devotion of the King Charles Spaniel is poignantly

A King Charles showing the breed's sense of fun.

David Barker

Sambo of Zubaida with son Sir Ivan and daughter Jessica.

Thomas Fall

illustrated by the little Blenheim called Blen, bred by Pauline Sharp, belonging to Bob Wood, the secretary of the King Charles Spaniel Club. On Bob's very sudden death Blen took up a vigil by the front door, as this was where he always waited for Bob's return from work. He simply would not believe his master was not coming back. Bob's wife tried to feed him by the door, but he refused all food, and veterinary attention was to no avail. He had lost the will to live. Blen, the gay extrovert, four-years-old, very soon joined his master. It is very hard not to be affected by such love and devotion, and it is one of the reasons why there is such a surge of interest in this very lovable, naughty and charming breed.

Late 19th Century
Postcards titled:
'The King's Own'
and 'Blenheim
Spaniel'

CHAPTER ONE

The History

> Happiest of the Spaniel race,
> Painter, with thy colours grace;
> Draw his forehead large and high,
> Draw his blue and humid eye;
> Draw his neck so smooth and round,
> Little neck with ribands bound;
> And the mutely swelling breast,
> Where the loves and Graces rest;
> And the spreading even back,
> Soft, and sleek, and glossy black;
> And the tail that gently twines,
> Like the tendrils of the vines;
> And the silky twisted hair,
> Shadowing thick the velvet ear;
> Velvet ears, which, hanging low,
> O'er the veiny temples flow.
>
> Swift

The Royal Toy Spaniels have been treasured through the ages in the royal houses of England and Europe. Indeed, King Charles II gave his royal title to his beloved toy spaniels, although the poor man seemed to be in constant trouble *'for playing with his dogs all the while, and not minding his business.'* Pepys also recorded on May 25, 1660: *'I went, and Mr Mansell, and one of the King's footmen, and a dog that the King loved, in a boat by ourselves, and so got on shore when the King did.'*

There are at least two recorded occasions when the unfortunate King had his dogs stolen, and he is reported to have written this impassioned plea himself:

'It is His Majesties own dog, and doubtless was stolen, for the dog was not born nor bred in England, and would never forsake His Master. Whosoever finds him may acquaint any at Whitehall for the dog was better known at Court,

than those who stole him. Will they never leave robbing His Majesty? Must he not keep a dog? This dog's place (though better than some imagine) is the only place which nobody offers to beg. June 28–July 5 1660.'

Just as they shared his life, so the little spaniels went on to share King Charles' death-bed, much to the consternation of the attending Bishop Burnet.

In 1613 Captain Saris is reported to have returned from Japan with small spaniels in an exchange of gifts and letters from the Emperor. The writer remarks on a similarity in size, shape and colour between the toy spaniels of the Eastern and Western Courts. Henrietta Maria, the sister of Charles II, also brought over her toy spaniels from the French courts, among them the little black-and-tan Pyrame, a small spaniel with fused feet, a legacy still inherited in our present day King Charles.

King James II, Charles' brother, obviously got his priorities right. When shipwrecked off the Scottish coast and compelled to abandon ship he ordered the crew: *'Save the dogs'*, and as an afterthought, *'and Colonel Churchill.'* The same Colonel Churchill later became Duke of Marlborough. Sara, Duchess of Marlborough, was said to have been so impatient for news of the battle of Blenheim that she constantly stroked the head of her little red and white spaniel. As the news of great victory was announced, the little spaniel gave birth to five little pups, allegedly bearing the Duchess's thumbprint on their skull. This became known as the Blenheim spot.

With their handsome appearance and lovable disposition, this imperious little breed has charmed its way through history. The noble Knight Fitz-Ralph, in the thirteenth century, returned from the Crusades to his home in Pebmarsh, Essex, bringing with him from a fishing village in Italy a strain of small, intelligent and beautiful spaniels. One can be seen at his feet in his effigy in the Parish Church. Dr Caius, physician to Queen Elizabeth I, described the spaniel as: *'little, pretty, and fyne, and sought for to satisfie the delicatenesse of daintie dames and wanton womens wills, instruments of folly for them to play and dally withall, to tryfle away the treasure of time, to withdraw their mindes from their commendable exercises. These puppies the small they be, the more pleasure they provoke are more meete play fellows for minsing mistresses to beare in their bosoms, to keepe company withall in their chambers, to succour with sleepe in bed, and nourishe with meate at board, to lie in their lappes.'* Dr Caius, true to the superstitions of the day, recommended that the Spaniell Gentle was able to soothe the sickness of the stomach. They should be worn as 'plasters' by sick and weakly people and with the warmth of the body the sickness transferred to the little dog and the patient became well and the little dog often died! A

Toy Spaniels: Covent Garden Charlie, Bawbee, Sepperl and Conrad.

Painting of two Late 19th Century King Charles Spaniels. Part of the Dreamridge Collection.

recommended cure for gout was a Spaniel puppy, two days old, boiled up with nettles, 'terpentyn, paramecete, olye of balm' and various secret drugs "to anoynt you where your grefe was".

Horace Walpole was another admirer of the King Charles Spaniel and in 1739, while doing the Grand Tour, he lost his beloved King Charles, Tony, to a marauding wolf high on an Alpine pass, when he stopped his chaise to take the air. Thereafter followed a succession of much-loved King Charles. Rosetta, a little black-and-tan, saved her master's life by warning him that the chimney was on fire. Another, Toutou, announced his arrival at Strawberry Hill by banishing Walpole's cat and instantly establishing his supremacy over the other dogs, receiving a bite on the foot for his pains. Nevertheless, he reigned supreme, dying at the age of sixteen. Along with Walpole's other King Charles', he was buried behind the chapel at Strawberry Hill.

The Reverend Idstone was a writer of the mid-Victorian period, and although he wrote a considerable treatise on the dogs of Great Britain, where he numbered the various breeds at forty, it is clear his heart lay with the King Charles Spaniel *'I have seen extraordinary instincts developed in these Spaniels. One, a dog in my possession in 1838, and until his death, was, from constant association with me and my friends, almost human; and as he held his head on one side, apparently endeavouring to fathom the meaning of conversation, it seemed as though he were almost prepared to join in it.*

'On one occasion he was sleeping in the room where a lady to whom he was much attached was moaning with pain, and, waking up, he seemed at a glance to understand the emergency, and, after a moment's consideration, endeavoured to pull the bell, though he had never before been taught to do so. Though impatient of strangers, he would at once permit the approaches of my friends at first sight, and more singular still, he understood and appreciated a dislike I did not venture to express, and would always dive at the legs of a couple of New College chaplains towards whom I had no cordiality. How did he know this, I wonder; or how divine that I had a sincere respect for Dr Pusey, to whom I never spoke in my life? – but such was the case, I am sure, by his manner and gestures, which, however, the sage never noticed or acknowledged.'

By the early nineteenth century the breed had evolved over the years to the present-day King Charles as we know it. By natural selection the face was shortened over a period of time. I do not believe any distinct cross was used or would have been necessary. The Royal Courts and Ducal houses all had their own strains of toy spaniels. In fact, one Duke of Norfolk used to feed his surplus King Charles pups to his pet eagles! Not only was the King Charles one of the favourite subjects of the Victorian artists, but the sixteenth century Italian artists such as Jacopo da Empoli and Veronese also used toy spaniels to embellish their work. There is a particularly attractive little spaniel with a beautifully domed head and low-set ears (the nose is a little longer than our present day King Charles but much shorter than the modern Cavalier) depicted in the Villa Maser. This was the home of the Contessa Marina Luling Buschetti, designed in 1560 by Palladio for Guisteniani Barbaro with frescoes and murals by Paolo Veronese. Signore Barbaro is shown with a nurse who is fondling this little Blenheim King Charles.

There have always been short-muzzled, round-headed little spaniels. Evolution and selective breeding over the centuries, culminating in the more intensive breeding of the nineteenth century, have set the standard we know today. Looking at the prints, woodcuts and photographs over the past hundred years, there has been very little change in the breed. Particularly if you compare these with the newly imported Pekingese of 1860 and the Pugs of that time: they would have been considered very long muzzled by today's standards, but the King Charles remains the same.

Just over a century ago, the first miniature dog shows began to be held between the working men in the East End taverns of London. Competition was keen and it was not unknown for these small spaniels to change hands from anywhere between £5 and £250. Mrs Jenkins, a well-known breeder at the turn of the century, with the Cleveden prefix, writes of visiting a Mr J. Garwood off Grays Inn Road in the 1860s. The old man lived quite alone except for the companionship of some twenty King Charles 'who shared equally with him, and who at his bidding, came out of mysterious corners and hiding.' Mrs Jenkins gives Mr Garwood the credit of being the source of the foundation stock of many of the best breeders at the turn of the century.

One of the most delightful stories I discovered in my research concerns one of the earliest champions, a Blenheim of some renown, who fathered quite a dynasty. From his picture, Bowsie looks a very attractive little dog. The story, which is told by his owner, illustrates the intelligence of breed.

'My old favourite would never make friends with any strangers, unless he considered them drawing-room guests; then he would don his most gracious airs, poise his head on one side, and put out his paw to be shaken, at the same time waving his flag in token of welcome. But woe be unto a backdoor intruder if Bowsie were near, no Bulldog or Mastiff could appear more formidable, and many time some unfortunate tradesman or tramp has rushed away, leaving a pattern of his most important garment in Mr Bowsie's teeth.

'Bowsie was a most sagacious dog. How dearly he loved a carriage drive, a railway journey, or a show! When the show hampers were brought out he would frisk and bark with delight, and would quickly open the lid with his tiny nose

Grace Darling and
Champion Bowsie.

Queen of the South.

and paw, and dive in, defying anyone but his mistress to remove him, and only then when assurance was given him that he would start for the show next day, could he be persuaded to come out to eat. On one occasion, when we were living in the country, Bowsie narrowly escaped being taken by express train to London. I had gone to town, and Bowsie, thinking that it was to a show, escaped from home by jumping from the window of an upper room, where he had been locked in for safety. He ran to the railway station, a distance of half a mile, and dashed into a first-class compartment of a train in waiting, where he complacently seated himself between two lady passengers. Fortunately, the station-master, seeing, and recognising my lord, sent him home safely, though crestfallen and disappointed.

'In the matter of food Bowsie was an epicure, and if one of his favourite dishes was on the table, and likely to be removed without his being served, he would sit with his back firmly planted against the door, defying the maid to pass with the dish, and tear her apron to ribbons should she dare the attempt. This little dog always went to bed with one of the children, and passed away at the age of fifteen, when he was sleeping in the arms of my youngest son. Never has there been a truer, more faithful friend than this animal, and although many years have passed since his death, I can scarcely keep the tears back as I write of him.'

Another famous champion of the early days was Lady Lytton's Ch Windfall, a pretty-headed Blenheim with a magnificent coat, a compact little dog with a gay, dancing action. He had two kennel-maids to attend to his needs. Like many of Lady Lytton's other dogs, he was taught to sneeze, growl, bark and whine to order. Windfall would also smile, shake his head for 'No' and nod for 'Yes'. A son of Windfall called Norrey (Ch Asffarel Windfall) would do elaborate tricks, such as threading his way round the legs of chairs or rolling from side to side to portray a ship in a rough sea; he would sham dead, play the piano and sing; he was also supposed to turn head over heels!

In 1885 a small band of devotees got together to form the Toy Spaniel Club. Each colour at that time was judged separately; the King Charles (Black and Tan), the Blenheim (Red and White), the Prince Charles (Tri-colour) and Ruby (Red). In October 1902 at a meeting of the Toy Spaniel Club held at the Crystal Palace, it was decided that, as all four varieties of English Toy Spaniel could be produced in one litter, they must all be the same family; and as the breed had existed with the historic name of King Charles Spaniel since the time of the Merry Monarch, they wished the club to be known as the King Charles Spaniel Club. The Kennel Club, on the other hand, wished to keep the name English Toy Spaniel, sub-divided by colour. An appeal was made by the powerful friends of the club to the King himself. His Majesty Edward VII let it be known to the Kennel Club that he wished the Toy Spaniel Club in future to be known by its historic name of the King Charles Spaniel Club. The Kennel Club naturally bowed to his royal wish. It is interesting to note that the early shows of 1885 mustered a mere couple of dozen dogs, but by 1904 the entry had risen to 109 dogs. The first official standard was adopted by the Toy Spaniel Club in 1885, and is illustrated with the woodcuts of the Victorian artist, Arthur Wardle.

1885 STANDARD

Head: This is the most prominent feature. 'It should be well domed, and in some specimens is absolutely semi-globular, sometimes even extending beyond the half-circle, and absolutely projecting over the eyes, so as to nearly meet the upturned nose.'

Eyes: These are set wide apart, with the eyelids square to the line of the face – not oblique, or fox-like. The eyes themselves are large, and so dark 'as to be generally considered black, their enormous pupils, which are absolutely of that colour, increasing the deception. From their large size, there is almost always a certain amount of weeping shown at the inner angles.' This is probably owing to the amount of light that enters in consequence, though it is said to be 'due to a defect in the lachrymal duct'.

Stop: The 'stop', or hollow between the eyes, is well marked, as in the Bulldog, or even more pronounced, some good specimens exhibiting a hollow deep enough to bury a small marble.

Nose: The nose must be short and well turned up between the eyes, and without any indication of artificial or unnatural displacement afforded by a deviation to either side. The colour of the end should be black, and it should be both deep and wide, with open nostrils.

Jaw: The lower jaw must be wide between its branches, leaving plenty of room for the tongue and for the attachment of the lower lips, which should completely conceal the teeth. It should be turned up, or 'finished', so as to allow of its meeting the end of the upper jaw, turned up in a similar way as above described. The tongue should on no account protrude.

Ears: The ears must be long, so as to approach the ground. In an average sized dog they measure 15 in to 20 in from tip to tip, and in some reach 22 in, or even more. They should be set low on the head, and heavily feathered. In this respect the King Charles is expected to exceed the Blenheim, and his ears occasionally extend to 24 ins.

Size: The most desirable size, according to the club standard, is determined by weight, which is 'from 7 lb to 10 lb'; but owing to the deceptive appearance of the small cobby dogs, 12 lb or 13 lb does not mean a large specimen.

Shape: In compactness of shape these Spaniels almost rival the Pug, but length of the coat adds greatly to the apparent bulk, as the body when the coat is wetted looks small in comparison with that dog. Still it ought to be decidedly 'cobby' with strong stout legs, broad back, and wide chest. The symmetry of the Toy Spaniel is of importance.

Coat: The coat should be long, silky, soft, and wavy but not curly. In the Blenheim, there should be a profuse mane, extending well down in front of the chest; and the feather should be displayed on the ears and feet, and so long as to give the latter the appearance of being webbed. It is also well carried up the back of the legs. In the King Charles, the feathering on the ears is very long and profuse, exceeding that of the Blenheim by an inch or more.

Tail: This is usually 'docked' to the length of 'three and a half or four inches'. The feather should be silky, and about five inches or six inches in length, constituting a marked 'flag', of a square shape, and not carried above the level of the back.

Colour: The King Charles is a rich glossy black and deep tan; tan spots over the eyes and on the cheeks and the usual markings on the legs are also required.

The Prince Charles or Tri-colour, should have the tan of the King Charles with markings like the Blenheim in black instead of red, on a pearly-white ground. The ears and under the tail should also be lined with tan. At present the Prince Charles requires no 'spot', that beauty having been reserved as the peculiar property of the Blenheim; but owing to the breed now being produced by a cross with the Blenheim, it is appearing and is considered a great acquisition, and will doubtless shortly be added as one of the 'points'.

The Ruby Spaniel is a rich chestnut-red. The presence of a few white hairs intermixed with the black on the chest of a King Charles, or intermixed with red on the chest of a Ruby Spaniel, shall carry great

Etchings to illustrate the original breed standard for the King Charles by Arthur Wardle 1864–1948.

Reproduction Thomas Fall.

King Charles: Blenheim.

"Our Dogs"

King Charles: Black and Tan.

King Charles: Ruby or Red.

King Charles: Tri-colour.

weight against a dog, but shall not itself actually disqualify; but a white patch on the chest or white on any other part of a King Charles or a Ruby Spaniel, shall be a disqualification. The colour of the nose to be black.

The Blenheim must on no account be whole-coloured, but should have a ground of pearly white, with bright rich chestnut or ruby-red markings, evenly distributed in large patches. The ears should be red, with a 'blaze' of white extending from the nose to the forehead, and ending in a crescent-shape curve. In the centre of this blaze there should be a clear 'spot of red', of the size of a sixpence.

SCALE OF POINTS

King Charles, Prince Charles, and Ruby Spaniels

Symmetry, Condition, and Size	20
Head	15
Stop	5
Muzzle	10
Eyes	10
Ears	15
Coat and Feathering	15
Colour	10
Total	100

Blenheim

Symmetry, Condition, and Size	15
Head	15
Stop	5
Muzzle	10
Eyes	10
Ears	10
Coat and Feathering	15
Colour and Markings	15
Spot	5
Total	100

CHAPTER TWO

Breed Standard of the King Charles Spaniel

General Appearance: Refined, compact and cobby.

Characteristics: Happy, intelligent, toy spaniel, with distinctive domed head.

Temperament: Reserved, gentle and affectionate.

Head and Skull: Skull large in comparison to size, well domed, full over eyes. Nose black with large, wide-open nostrils, very short and turned up to meet skull. Stop between skull and nose well defined. Muzzle square, wide and deep, well turned up, lower jaw wide, lips exactly meeting, giving nice finish. Cheeks not falling away under eyes, but well cushioned.

Eyes: Very large and dark, set wide apart, eyelids block square to face line, pleasing expression.

Ears: Set on low, hanging quite flat to cheeks, very long and well feathered.

Mouth: Bite should be slightly undershot. Protruding tongue highly undesirable.

Neck: of medium length; arched, giving proud carriage of head.

Forequarters: Legs short, straight. Shoulders well laid back, elbows close to rib cage, turning neither in nor out.

Body: Chest wide and deep, back short and level.

Hindquarters: Sufficient muscle to give positive driving movement, stifles well bent, hocks well let down and defined. Straight viewed from behind, turning neither in nor out.

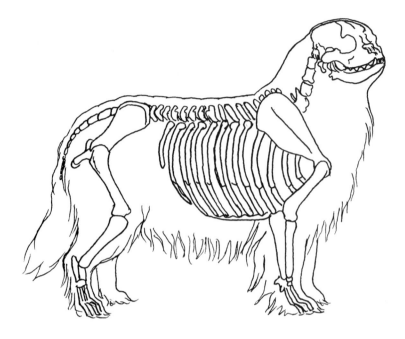

Skeletal outline.

Incorrect angulation.

Feet: Compact, well padded and feathered, toes well knuckled, round cat-shaped foot, well cushioned, pasterns firm. Occasionally central pad and nails fused together.

Tail: Well feathered, not carried over or above level of back. Docking optional.

Gait/Movement: Free, active and elegant, driving from behind. Sound movement highly desirable.

Coat: Long, silky and straight, slight wave allowed, never curly. Legs, ears and tail profusely feathered.

Colour: Black and Tan: Rich glossy black, with bright mahogany tan markings on muzzle, legs, chest, linings of ears, under tail and spots over eyes. White patch on chest undesirable.
Tricolour: Ground pearly white, with well distributed black patches, brilliant tan markings on cheeks, linings of ears, under tail and spots over eyes. Wide white blaze between eyes and up forehead.
Blenheim: Ground pearly white, with well distributed chestnut red patches. Wide clear blaze with the 'spot' in centre of skull, should be a clear chestnut red mark about the size of a penny.
Ruby: Whole coloured, rich chestnut red. White patch on chest highly undesirable.

Size: Weight: 3.6-6.3 kg (8-14 lbs).

Faults: Any departure from the foregoing points should be considered a fault and the seriousness with which the fault should be regarded should be in exact proportion to its degree.

Note Male animals should have two apparently normal testicles fully descended into the scrotum.

This is the standard revised by the Kennel Club in 1985 after the three breed clubs had each submitted their suggestions. Over the years since the first standard was drawn up by the Toy Spaniel club in 1885 taken from Stonehenge, there has been little mention of soundness, unfortunately to the detriment of the breed. Nevertheless the King Charles Spaniel, although a toy dog and companion par excellence, should be capable of living a normal life, and I for one am delighted that the section

*Ch Curtana Morgana
illustrating the perfect
dome head and soft
expression.*

Gait/Movement now reads: 'Free, active, and elegant, driving from behind. Sound movement highly desirable.' The appearance of strength in the hindquarters depends on the placement of the leg in relation to hip and bend of stifle, the positioning and length of the hock, and in being free of luxating patellas and slack hocks. Patellar luxation is indicated by a quick snatching of the hocks giving a short, choppy stride or sometimes a skipping action as it passes the supporting leg and twists the rear pastern in beneath the body. The problem may be present on one side only (unilateral), or affect both sides (bilateral), and occurs if the dog is born with a groove which is abnormally shallow. Unfortunately, this condition is hereditary and its mode of inheritance makes it extremely difficult to eradicate. To a very large degree, the action of a King Charles depends upon the shape and placement of the shoulder blades. The shoulder should be well laid back and of good length. The two blades should be close together on top, not wide apart, which would give a loaded appearance. A good shoulder produces a long free action with a good length of stride which covers the ground in the most economical and effective manner possible.

The body of a King Charles should have a wide deep chest, well ribbed. At no time should it be short of rib, or have deformed ribs or even lack ribs: all these must be regarded as serious structural weaknesses. The back should be short and level. The front legs should be short, straight and well boned, with compact feet turning neither in nor out. Two types of foot are acceptable: the round cat-shaped foot and the central pad fused together: (usually the nails are fused as well but not always). Sometimes all four feet have the centrally fused pad, sometimes just one or two.

The docking of King Charles Spaniels is optional: as a result some dogs appear with a small lump or twist in the tail. The importance lies with the carriage of the tail, which should not be carried over the level of the back in terrier fashion. Complete absence of a tail is a serious genetic fault: the tail is the continuation of the dog's spine. A fully feathered, active, and merry tail should be an attractive feature of the King Charles denoting its happy temperament and joy of life.

The head of the King Charles Spaniel is his crowning glory, characterised by the domed head and short face. The skull, though domed, should not be of such excessive proportions as to give rise to idiocy or hydrocephalus (water on the brain), and there should never be a molero, a hole in the centre of the skull due to incomplete fusion of the frontal bones. The muzzle should be thoroughly well-cushioned up each side of the nose. When looked at in front, the muzzle should form a perfect arch, which puffs out on each side of the nose.

The whole face of a King Charles Spaniel should have a round, chubby, furry appearance and a sweet, pretty, melting expression, with no lines, furrows or irregularities of outline. At no time should the nose be so short that it appears to be sunk into the skull; you should be able to lay a pencil across the top of a King Charles's nose. The nostrils should never be pinched; the top of the nose must be on a level with the eyes. The eyes, which must be dark and gentle in expression, must be set absolutely straight, but not so wide apart that they appear to be set on the side of the head. The underjaw should have plenty of width between the canine teeth and must not at any time appear too strong and protrude right out beyond the upper lip. A King Charles should never have an ugly expression. The long silky ears frame the face. The whole head is set on a good arched neck, giving the proud aristocratic bearing required.

Temperament is of utmost importance: the standard stresses the intelligence and the happy nature of the King Charles. The King Charles is lively, extremely intelligent, capricious, full of fun and very trainable. But there is a tenuous connection between temperament and movement. The dog whose conformation is of the kind which makes it difficult for him to move, shows his resentment of the discomfort he is experiencing by refusing to move or by moving erratically. However, the most perfectly proportioned dog may be a failure in the show ring if he does not align himself mentally with his owner's requirements and cannot co-operate in activities that may seem natural to his owner's expectations but which seems incomprehensible to him. The show ring is therefore an excellent guide to breeders for both temperament and type.

The long silky coat and beautifully feathered ears are very much a feature of the adult King Charles. The white in the broken colours should be the pearly white hue that sparkles silver in the sunlight. The tan should be rich mahogany red in the Rubies and Blenheims, and the black should be shiny deep raven. The richness of the colours of the King Charles is very much a feature of the breed.

The perfect King Charles is the composite of all the ideals laid out in the standard, plus quality. What is quality? Lady Lytton says: *'Quality is the most difficult thing in the world to explain to those who do not instinctively recognise it. It is an intangible something which does not depend entirely upon line, but upon a combination of lines, thickness, width, breadth, deep curve, etc, and their relation to one another; the result producing to the eye, without any conscious mental effort, a certain perfection and exquisiteness without which mere dull correctness is lifeless and uninteresting.*

'It is the difference between coarse linen and fine cambric, or let us say, between good and bad cooking, where the ingredients may all be the same, yet

the result right in one case and wrong in the other. Dogs may be made of the same component points, and yet they may be indefinably wrong. Just as you make out recipes for a bad cook in vain, you may compile standards until you are tired. Nothing will avail you unless your judge can recognise quality.

Quality gives a certain brilliance; a dog with quality strikes the eye, though he may be doing nothing in particular. You may only catch a glimpse of him, or he may be lying fast asleep, yet you cannot help noticing him. In movement he has a certain pride of carriage, a certain exquisiteness of colour, a certain beauty, in fact, which others equally good in points have not.

'Quality cannot be defined in standards or divided into scales, but, like beauty and genius in the human race, it must remain forever independent of legislation.'

Tudorhurst Rebecca: An outstanding example of quality.

Thomas Fall

Ch Tudorhurst
Royal Rebellion.

Thomas Fall

In my ideal standard the King Charles Spaniel is built on refined lines (with the typical build and balance of a Spaniel). It should be compact and cobby, the back short and level, with good depth of body and spring of ribs; free and sound on the move, giving a general impression of elegance and quality which is enhanced by the profuse coat and feathering. The head is large and domed, the face short with the lips meeting evenly to give a good finish to the mouth. Eyes round, large and dark, set in square to the face to give a sweet and lively expression. The whole head is framed by the long, low-set and profusely feathered ears. The legs are of medium length, well-boned and straight, with hocks and stifles well bent and toes turned neither in nor out. The King Charles is essentially a sound spaniel of toy size. In character he is merry and active, with a happy temperament.

Head Studies.

The head should be massive in comparison to size of the dog, well-domed and full over the eyes. Nose black with large wide open nostrils. The mouth should be somewhat undershot with the lower jaw protruding slightly beyond the upper. Jaws to meet evenly and teeth to be strong, white and regular with good width between the canine teeth. The lips, which should be black in all colours, to just cover the teeth giving a neat finish to the mouth, upper lips to be somewhat full to give a well cushioned finish to the foreface.

The turn-up of the lower jaw should not be too abrupt and it must not project too far in front of the top of the face, a wide soft curve is what is wanted. The top of the lower jaw, the tip of the nose and the frontal part of the skull above the eyes should all be in line, with the nose short and well up between the eyes, but not so short as to conceal the stop. Narrow jaws, wry mouth or protruding tongue are most objectionable. The eyes should be round, dark and large but not bolting, set wide apart and square to the line of face – never obliquely. Light eyes are most undesirable, entropion a serious fault. Ears are set on low and should hang quite flat to cheeks, very long and feathered.

Correct eye and nose placement.

Eyes set on the side of the skull.

*Muzzle not square, lower jaw
narrow, cheeks not filled.*

*Eyes too high, upper lips
too loose and falling together.*

Showing tongue.

Under-jaw too strong.

Ears set too high.

Head too flat.

Jawlines: King Charles

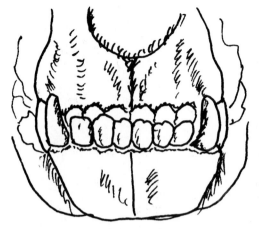

Undershot, viewed
from the front,
correct according to
the breed standard.

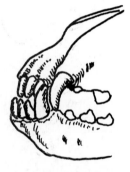

Undershot, viewed
from the side.

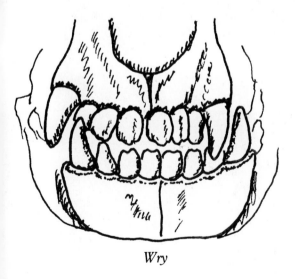

Wry

(a)   *(b)*

Pads: (a) Cat-like, (b) Fused toes.

A dog with incorrect angulation taking short, stilted strides.

A dog with correct angulation covering the ground with balanced strides.

The movement should be gay, free and lively – straight and true, front and back, elbows and feet the same distance apart when approaching and hocks not too close together or far apart when going away.

Cow hocks, bowed hocks and slipping patellas are all serious faults.

In profile movement there should be a good length of stride, drive from the hocks with a proud carriage of the head, no dipping of the backline or hind quarters.

The body should be short and cobby, well ribbed up, chest wide and deep down to the elbow with a short, broad and level back, loins short and strong. In a well-balanced mature dog the depth from the top of shoulder to the brisket should be about the same as the length of the foreleg and the length from the shoulder to the root of the tail about the same as from the shoulder to the ground.

Temperament is a most important feature and should always take precedence over minor faults. The King Charles should be gay, gentle, lively, sweet tempered, affectionate and intelligent with plenty of spirit but responsive to control. He is an aristocrat and should always show quality and balance in both body structure and temperament. Nervousness is a serious fault.

Joshua & Jeremiah of Jarrah. Two Blenheims showing quality and substance.

Ideally the tail should be straight and fine, well feathered, set on slightly below the line of the back, as in all spaniels, and carried gaily but not above the line of the back and should wag ceaselessly on the move. Docking is optional but if docked the length should be in balance with the length of the body. Absence of tail is a serious fault as it may affect the bodily functions. The coat should be long, silky and straight. A slight wave allowed – not curly. The legs, ears and tail should be profusely feathered.

The neck should be of good length and arched to give a proud carriage of the head, shoulders and upper arms well laid back in typical spaniel manner to give freedom of movement and a good length of stride. Elbows close to the side, never protruding. Forelegs to have good bone, they should be of medium length and perfectly straight from any angle, smooth in front and well feathered at the back. Feet well padded and feathered, toes compact and well knuckled up. (The fused foot sometimes seen is not untypical.) Pasterns should be firm and feet turn neither in nor out, standing or moving.

The hindquarters should be well boned with sufficient muscle to give positive driving movement. Stifles well bent, hocks well let down and defined, straight and sound, turning neither in nor out. Hind feet are somewhat smaller than forefeet. There is profuse feathering on the back of the hind legs.

Correct.

Cow hocks.

Too wide.

Too narrow.

Hocks too long.

Bone too fine.

Correct.

Pigeon-toed.

Too narrow.

East-West.

Bowed.

Chippendale.

CHAPTER THREE

The King Charles in the 20th Century

WITH so little change in breed type over the past one hundred years, we must be grateful to the dedicated breeders who preserved the breed through two world wars and kept going in difficult circumstances to emerge with a nucleus of quality dogs. Two of the greatest prefixes, the Ashtonmore of Mrs Raymond Mallock and the Lavenderway of Mrs E.H. Mitchell, were both founded before the first World War. In 1920 Lady Fowler of Braemore started a kennel that produced many typical and beautiful dogs. Mr Whiting's black and tans and rubies were of very high quality; his Ch Little Minaster and Ch Gina of Minaster were outstanding. Other prominent breeders were Lady de Gex and Miss Ella Brunne, famous for the Hentzau prefix.

In 1924 the Duke of Marlborough gave Mrs Raymond Mallock a truly beautiful flat-faced Blenheim, richly marked and complete with the Blenheim spot. This became the great Ch Ashtonmore Crusader. He was known as Toby on the Blenheim estate where he was bred and raised, and all our present-day King Charles go back to him in some marked degree. On the death of Mrs Raymond Mallock, Mrs Clayton Swan of Barhams Manor purchased Ch Ashtonmore Lovesong, an exquisite Blenheim, whose parents were Ch Ashtonmore Cupid and the outstanding bitch Ch Ashtonmore Wildflower. According to Mrs Clayton Swan, he was as charming as he was beautiful. When Mrs Raymond Mallock's kennel was dispersed, Mrs Clayton Swan also purchased Ashtonmore Malise, a half-brother to Lovesong through Ch Ashtonmore Cupid. Malise, like his sire Cupid, was to make his mark on the breed. Mrs Mitchell put Malise to Molliecoddle of Lavenderway, a granddaughter of Ch Ashtonmore Cupid, and in April 1942 the great Ch Michael of Lavenderway was born. Michael was not only a beautiful dog in his own right, he had the ability to pass on these attributes to his progeny. If Michael had been born ten years later he would not have gained his title and possibly he would not have been used so extensively at stud, for he was a unilateral cryptorchid. In those days this was not considered a hereditary fault. In 1944 Mrs Mitchell

Ch Challenger 1912 owned by Lady Lytton.

Thomas Fall

Ashtonmore King Charles – pictured left to right, Ch Ashtonmore Domino, Ch Ashtonmore Crystal, Ch Ashtonmore Crusader, Ch Ashtonmore Wildflower, Ch Ashtonmore Barritone.

Thomas Fall

bred from Molliecoddle of Lavenderway again, this time using Boniface of St Lucia, a great-great-grandson of Ch Ashtonmore Barritone and again a great-great-grandson of Ch Ashtonmore Cupid. Incidentally, Cupid was a son of my original pin-up girl, Ch Braemore Cherry. This union produced Ch Jasper of Lavenderway, a lovely Blenheim, owned by Mrs Violet Pond of the Breda King Charles.

Jasper sired many lovely King Charles for Mrs Pond, who was always very grateful to Mrs Mitchell for letting her have the dog. Ch Serena of Breda, Ch Osbaston Jeanette of Breda, and my own particular favourite, Ch Celia of Breda, and Ch Troubadour Glazert were all bred by Mrs Pond and sired by Jasper. Mrs Pond adored her King Charles but always viewed the mating and whelping with fear and trepidation. At her request, Miss D.V. Vincent officiated at the early matings of Ch Jasper and as a thank-you present Miss Vincent was given Julian of Breda, a son of Ch Jasper and Penelope of Breda herself, a daughter of Miss Vincent's Ch Rupert of Vihurst. When Julian was mated to Ch Falaise of Vihurst, a granddaughter of Ch Roderick of Lavenderway, she produced the outstanding Blenheim, Ch Pierre Again of Vihurst, whose career in the show ring spanned eleven years and included a tally of twenty-one challenge certificates. After Miss Vincent's kindness to her, Mrs Pond felt she had to do the deed herself. An accomplished pianist, she said she used to put the two King Charles on the chesterfield while she played the Moonlight Sonata and let nature take its course! For many years Mrs Pond was a gracious and charming president of the King Charles Spaniel Club and was a very treasured friend.

In 1968 Mrs Pond wrote this charming article on the death of her dear friend Miss Aline Doxford, who was a leading figure in the breed.

'To most of you she meant just a name behind a cup, but during the Forties and Fifties when I was showing, she took a great interest in the club as patron – literally showering gifts of silver to be won outright by members.

At the beginning of the century the prefix Ruritania related to hounds – Wolfhounds, Deerhounds and Salukis – which became famous winners, but later as she grew older her interest was in smaller dogs. After Pekingese came the King Charles and for the past twenty-two years my Charlies were her sole companions.

At one time there were seven of them at Silksworth, where they spent a life of ease and freedom in the lovely house and gardens. All day long they stayed in a drawing-room, full of cabinets of jade, ivories, china and Fabergé pieces of pet dogs. They were never bred from and could have graced any show.

Being a strict adherent to the American-inspired 'Hay' diet, which does not mix acids and starches at the same meal, Miss Doxford extended the idea to her

Ch Braemore Cherry owned and bred by Lady Fowler, 1931. Thomas Fall

Ch Berceuse of Braemore owned and bred by Lady Fowler. Thomas Fall

Ch Ashtonmore Magda 1934.
Thomas Fall

Ch Roderick of Lavenderway 1938. Thomas Fall

*Ashtonmore King
Charles Spaniels
1937.*

Thomas Fall

dogs, who were fed on raw minced meat night and morning, with the starch meal (biscuits) at 4 pm. This was taken, weather permitting, in the garden house with all seven 'Pondites' (her nickname for them) sitting round a trestle table on wicker tub chairs with their nightcaps on so that they did not eat their ears with their biscuits. Their ears and coats literally swept the ground. The nightcaps were made of very fine muslin with thin elastic each side, and when the dogs were let out of their sleeping boxes in the library each morning it was the quaintest sight to see the row of little heads with caps sticking up from them.

By 1966 the last of them died (all lived till they were in their teens) and I went up again for the last visit, to give Miss Doxford my black and tan Chloe for companionship. She adored her, and Chloe was a great comfort to her in her last days on earth; now she is back again with me and giving the same devotion. I remember years ago, when I first bought King Charles, a friend said, 'But Violet, they are dowagers' dogs', and so they may well be, for I know of no other breed that I would, like Miss Doxford, prefer to share my last years with.'

Miss Vincent bred many great dogs but her favourite was Ch Pierre Again. Both Mrs Violet Jackson of the Homehursts and Mrs White of the Blueshadows combined the Lavenderway and Vihurst bloodlines to produce their winners. Ch Elizabeth of Homehurst, a beautiful-headed tri-colour with a superb body and movement, was by Ch Rupert of Vihurst, a grandson of Ch Roderick of Lavenderway. Her dam, Carol Anne of Homehurst, was a granddaughter of Ch Michael of Lavenderway. Mrs Jackson, Mrs Pond and Miss Vincent had a friendship spanning fifty years – in fact Miss Vincent and Mrs Jackson had been childhood companions – but they always called each other Miss Vincent, Mrs Pond and Mrs Jackson. To use the familiarity of Christian names would have been unthinkable! Mrs Jackson is particularly dear to my heart, as without her help there would have been no Tudorhursts.

The mid-Forties and Fifties saw dogs bearing the pre-war prefix of St Lucia, belonging to Mrs Mabel Gristwood, hitting the headlines. Ch Mary Rose of St Lucia, Ch Sandycuft Julia of St Lucia, Ch Clarissa of St Lucia, Ch Goldendays Galiard Rose of St Lucia and Ch Goldendays Penn Rose of St Lucia are just a few of the champions bred by Mrs Gristwood. In 1958 Mrs Gristwood bred a black and tan, Tudor Minstrel of St Lucia, sired by Regency Beau of St Lucia out of Rock and Roll of St Lucia. He was an outstanding dog, well-made and very sound. I am sure Mrs Gristwood remembers the day of Birmingham National at Bingley Hall in 1962 when Tudor Minstrel won the challenge certificate. Realising we were running late with judging we fled out of Bingley Hall to catch a taxi to Birmingham Snowhill Station. The train was delayed so we decided to walk our dogs on the platform. When Mrs Gristwood opened her hamper, it was empty! She

*Mrs Clayton Swan's
Ch Ashtonmore
Lovesong and Milo
of Barhams 1941.*

Thomas Fall

*Mrs Violet Pond
with Annette and
Lancelot of Breda.*

Tudor Photos

Leo Wilson awarding BOB to Ch Pierre Again of Vihurst at Hove Ch Show 1954 with Ch Goldendays Penn Rose of St Lucia BOS.

Mrs D.V. Jackson's Ch Elizabeth of Homehurst (Ch Rupert of Vihurst – Carol Anne of Homehurst) 23.10.47.

Thomas Fall

had to make a quick return visit to Bingley Hall to collect the newly-crowned, rather aggrieved champion who was still sitting on his bench!

In 1945 Mrs Dalton bred a bitch called Betty of Hatherleigh. She was by Christopher of St Lucia and Arcadian Charm, an Ashtonmore Cupid granddaughter. This tri-colour was purchased by Mrs Mollie Castle as the foundation of the Oakridges. She ultimately gained her title in 1951. In 1948 Betty of Hatherleigh produced a litter to Gouldesborough David, a son of Peter of Vihurst and Blueshadow Harmony. From this union came Sweet Memory of Oakridges, who gained her championship in 1953. Mrs Castle found a successful combination using Shamus of Old Rowley, a strong-headed Blenheim dog owned by Mrs Madge Weston. He was a grandson of Ch Hurleston Peterson of Lavenderway who was a Blenheim dog bred by Mrs White of the Blueshadow prefix, himself a son of Peter of Vihurst. The dam, English Rose of Oakridges, was also a Peter of Vihurst great granddaughter. This produced Ch Rapture of Oakridges. From a grandson of Rapture Mrs Castle produced Ch Goldspot of Oakridges. Posy, Goldspot's mother, was another great granddaughter of Peter's. Ch Comforter, Ch Una, Ch Tranquillity and Ch Laundra, as well as Ch Isobelle and Ch Prince Regent, all came from these lines and played their part in the make-up of the famous Oakridges kennel. Mrs Castle's Oakridges have always been synonymous with beautiful heads, substantial bodies and good bone. Forty years on, the Oakridges still continue.

Another clever and talented breeder of the Forties and Fifties was Mrs Winifred Darrcott of Thatchend King Charles. Ch Philemon of Thatchend, a son of Ch Michael of Lavenderway, was the sire of Mrs Roger Cooper's Ch Roger of Louisdor and Ch Alexandra of Thatchend owned by Mrs Gristwood. Coppernob of Thatchend, a son of Peter of Vihurst, appears in many pedigrees. In fact, Coppernob was mated to his own daughter and produced Ch Charlotte of Thatchend.

Mrs Eve Chisholm purchased Rosemary of Thatchend, a daughter of Ch Charlotte of Thatchend by Ch Philemon. In 1952 Rosemary was mated to Peregrine of Thatchend, another Ch Michael son, and the result was Ch Goldendays Gay Galliard. In turn, Gay Galliard sired Ch Goldendays Galliard Rose of St Lucia who was out of Mrs Gristwood's Ch Mary Rose of St Lucia, and when mated with Sunmaid of Ilkleyview, a Ch Roger of Louisdor daughter, Galliard produced the exquisite Ch Goldendays Gay Venture, but sadly he was sterile.

In 1958 Mrs Chisholm purchased Cyrus of Lavenderway who became Ch Goldendays Cyrus of Lavenderway. His litter brother, Lucian of

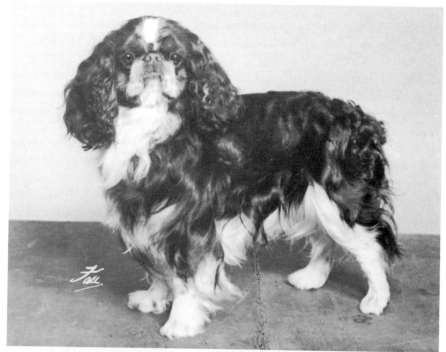

Alicia Pennington's Ch Homehurst Merry Monarch bred by Mrs D.V. Jackson. (Ch Goldendays Cyrus of Lavenderway – Charleen Tu of Homehurst). 1959.

Thomas Fall

Mrs Mabel Gristwood's Ch Tudor Minstrel of St Lucia 1964. (Regency Beau of St Lucia – Rock and Roll of St Lucia). 3.6.58.

Thomas Fall

Lavenderway, was purchased by Mrs Joyce Birchall, and litter sister Araminta of Lavenderway was bought by Mrs Corder of the Carwyns prefix. An earlier litter, similarly bred, had produced Ch Juliana of Lavenderway for Mrs White of the Blueshadow prefix. Mrs White mated Juliana to Cyprion of St Lucia, a Rex and Unity of Lavenderway grandson, and five tri-colour dog pups were born. All were of outstanding quality but only one pup was entire, Ch Blueshadow Ricardo, and no progeny resulted from him. In 1962 Mrs White was near to breeding her last litter of Blueshadow King Charles. Ch Juliana had been mated again, this time to a Regency Beau – Ch Clarissa son, Little Lovelace of St Lucia. The result was Blueshadow Jacqueline, a lovely tri-colour who never gained the title she deserved. When she was mated to Ch Goldendays Cyrus of Lavenderway she produced Ch Blueshadow Cresta and Mrs Keswick's Pargeter Blueshadow Christina. Shortly after Cresta gained her title in 1967, Mrs White retired to live with her sister and later died, but not before Blueshadow Jacqueline had a litter to Ch Karim of Ainsleyfield, producing the final of a long line of Blueshadows.

Another outstanding Blenheim grandson of Ch Michael of Lavenderway was Jan of Jarrah. Owned and bred by the Misses Turner sisters, Jan had two challenge certificates to his credit when the Kennel Club ruling came in forbidding the entry of unilateral cryptorchids (monorchid). Jan was used extensively at stud and sired Ch Milescroft Trudy Trot and Ch Troutburn Janissary of Jarrah. Janina of Jarrah, a daughter of Jan, was mated to Mrs Gristwood's Mountcharles Sultan. This produced the famous Jarrah twins, Joshua and Jeremiah. Joshua of Jarrah produced Ch Pargeter Palamina for Mrs Keswick. In turn, Palamina was mated to Pargeter Clover, a grandson of Ch Troutburn Janissary of Jarrah, and she produced Ch Marchris Bertie Boy for Mrs Elinor Martin.

Mrs Pauline Sharp of the Zubaida King Charles had another grandson of Ch Michael of Lavenderway, Sandycuft Glamour Boy. Glamour Boy was full brother to Mrs Chisholm's Ch Wild Boy of Sandycuft. Glamour Boy was put to his daughter Ch Wild Orchid of Zubaida, a quite exquisite tri-colour, and produced the very lovely Ch Rambler of Zubaida owned by Mrs Josephine Rouse. Wild Orchid's litter brother was the glamorous silky-coated Blenheim, Stuart King of Zubaida. Mrs Sharp retained Ch Rambler's litter sister, Wild Rose of Zubaida. She, in turn, was mated to her half-brother Homehurst Tudor King, who had been recently purchased by Mrs Madeline Harper. Wild Rose produced seven puppies, one of whom was my own Royal Richard of Zubaida. When Mrs Chisholm died, it was her wish that Ch Goldendays Homehurst Gay Royal, litter

Mrs Winifred Darracott's Ch Hurlestone Peterson of Lavenderway bred by Mrs D.E. White (Peter of Vihurst – Blueshadow Harmony) 31.4.47.

Mrs M. Castle's Ch Laundra of Oakridges (Sweet Rapture of Oakridges – Oakridges Posy of Jordans) 2.11.60.

M. Cooke and Son

*Mrs Eve Chisholm
and some of the
Goldendays.*

D.G. Davis

brother to Homehurst Tudor King, should go to Mrs Sharp. Another son of Sandycuft Glamour Boy was Mrs Rouse's Ch Karim of Ainsleyfield. Karim's dam was a granddaughter of Ch Elizabeth of Homehurst – Jacqueline of Homehurst. Mrs Rouse mated Tamara of Ainsleyfield, litter sister to Ch Karim, to her half-brother Stuart King of Zubaida; the result was my Blenheim, Tudorhurst Rhapsody of Ainsleyfield.

Pauline and Stanley Sharp helped many newcomers to the breed and it was not long before their neighbours in Patcham, Brighton, had fallen for King Charles Spaniels. Norman and Betty Brown, with the help of Pauline Sharp, started the Castleray King Charles about 1970. In 1973 they bred their first champion, Ch Castleray Emma, a very pretty Bleinheim, always shown in beautiful coat. Her dam was a daughter of Ch Goldendays Homehurst Gay Royal and her sire Ch Tudorhurst Simon.

In 1956 Mrs Joyce Birchall announced the opening of her Zepherine kennel. From Mrs Pauline Sharp she purchased the foundation of her whole-colour line, Bunty of Zubaida, as well as appearing in her broken-colour line. Bunty of Zubaida was a ruby, sired by Mrs Sharp's ruby dog, Goldust of Thatchend, out of a little Blenheim interbred Toy Spaniel, Kuchick Oman. Bunty was mated to Red Call of St Lucia and produced Zepherine Cuckoo, a lovely Blenheim bitch, the foundation of the Cuckoo line. Another of Mrs Birchall's foundation bitches was Zepherine Beaucourt Little Witch. When she was mated to Ch Rapture of Oakridges she produced Zepherine Villette and Zepherine Moby Dick for Mrs Birchall and Sweet Rapture of Oakridges for Mrs Castle. Lucian of Lavenderway was mated to Zepherine Villette and produced Zepherine Phineas, the sire of Gilpin, also Zepherine Dombey and Patience. Many breeders have used Gilpin as the cornerstone of their breeding. Mrs Birchall bred her first champion, Zepherine Clement, in 1967, a very lovely cobby tri-colour full of personality. He won twenty-six challenge certificates and made many friends for the breed. He was owned and exhibited by Mrs Freda Scivers. Mrs Scivers also owned Ch Zepherine Viola who was bred by Roy Davies in 1966. She was out of Zepherine Sara, a Bunty of Zubaida and Ch Goldendays Cyrus of Lavenderway granddaughter, by his Graslon Royal Velvet, a Zepherine Patience daughter and Lucian of Lavenderway granddaughter. Over the years Roy Davies has consistently bred many good dogs for Mrs Birchall, some in his own prefix of Graslon but many carrying the Zepherine prefix. The most famous being Ch Graslon Aphrodite.

In 1971 Mr Neal Beck bred Ch Oakorange Goldilocks, a ruby by Zepherine Sirius out of their homebred Oakorange Wistaria, a daughter of Zepherine Cresside, similarly bred to Zepherine Clement. Mrs Birchall was a strong advocate of line-breeding and in particular admired the Lavenderway line. She was certainly not alone in her admiration. She held very strong views and was never afraid to voice them. In 1970 she wrote: *'Winning dogs are invariably under fire from people, perhaps through ignorance of the breeding or envy. One little word to the denigrators: all our dogs today stem from the lines Lavenderway, Vihurst, Blueshadow and the two whole colours Gilbert of Louisdor and Flame of Ainsdale. Our present dogs have evolved according to the knowledge and/or desire of the breeders, not always perhaps with the Standard stamped on the inner eye, or the knowledge of inherited faults, which call for test breeding and culling, things which I have often written about.*

If you run down two dogs of similar origin, you condemn both. For if one dog has all the faults, so will the other. Inherited factors for good or bad will be carried by both dogs. When dogs meet continually and change place, it is no more than what the eye on each occasion sees. And no two people see exactly the same, but constant winning proves that they are very similar.'

In 1959 Carolyn of Homehurst, a beautiful tri-colour daughter of Ch Elizabeth of Homehurst, came to live with me. From her daughter Charleen Tu of Homehurst we had Ch Homehurst Merry Monarch and

Mrs Mollie Castle's Ch Corosco Peerless Peter of Oakridges breeder Mrs Corlett (Ch Huntglen Darcy – Laureats Nina) 3.12.71.

Pearce

Homehurst Merry Maid. The original much-treasured line has remained unbroken. Merry Maid had two litters. One was to Ch Karim of Ainsleyfield (a Carolyn grandson) which produced Tudorhurst Princess Aurora and Australian Ch Tudorhurst Fair Maid, the other to Royal Richard of Zubaida giving us Tudorhurst Thumbelina (two challenge certificates). From Aurora and Tudorhurst Firebird, a tri-colour son of Merry Princess, came Tudorhurst Tabitha and Tudorhurst Thomasina, two bitches who made their mark on the breed. In Scandinavia, Finnish and Swedish, Ch Tudorhurst Trojan Warrior carried the flag, and, in Australia, it was Australian Ch Tudorhurst Tarantella.

Ch Homehurst Merry Monarch and Tudorhurst Rhapsody of Ainsleyfield (a granddaughter of Carolyn) produced Ch Tudorhurst Son of Monarch, the sire of Australian Ch Tudorhurst Jester of Jarrah, and the

Zepherine Gilpin, the kingpin of the Zepherine Kennels (Zepherine Phineas – Goldendays Jacquasta). Owner/breeder: Mrs Birchall.

Mrs Freda Sciver's Ch Zepherine Clement bred by Mrs Joyce Birchall (Zepherine Gilpin – Zepherine Claudette) 15.7.67 Thomas Fall

outstanding brood Ch Tudorhurst Merry Princess. Her first litter to Ch Goldendays Homehurst Gay Royal (another grandson of Carolyn) produced Ch Tudorhurst Snow Queen and Tudorhurst Firebird; her second to Joshua of Jarrah produced Ch Tudorhurst Jane. Some of Jane's direct descendants include USA Ch Tudorhurst Julius, USA Ch Tudorhurst Josephine and Ch Larkrise Red Robin. Merry Princess's final litter to Royal Richard of Zubaida, a son of Homehurst Tudor King and litter brother of Gay Royal, produced Ch Tudorhurst Rebecca. Tudorhurst Serenade, full sister to Merry Princess, produced Ch Tudorhurst Simon (sire Zepherine Gilpin). Another litter sister was Australian Ch Tudorhurst Sonata. When Rebecca was mated to Ch Zepherine Clement she produced Ch Tudorhurst Rowena, and when she was put to Simon the result was Ch Tudorhurst Royal Rebellion. From Rebellion came Ch Tudorhurst Royal Revenge who was out of the ruby, Zepherine Carmen, and from Rebellion and Tabitha came Ch Tudorhurst Toreador (the great grandsire of Ch Moordown Morning Glory of Tudorhurst). Toreador's litter brother was the Swedish and Finnish Ch Tudorhurst Trojan Warrior, and litter sister to Tudorhurst Teazel, dam of Ch Tudorhurst Royal Command, whose sire was Tudorhurst Royal Captive, a son of Rebecca.

Ch Tudorhurst Jane (Joshua of Jarrah – Ch Tudorhurst Merry Princess) 7.11.68.

Thomas Fall

*Ch Tudorhurst
Royal Revenge (Ch
Tudorhurst Royal
Rebellion –
Zepherine Carmen)
14.6.76.*

Thomas Fall

*Julia Huggins' Ch
Curtana Legend
(Maplehurst
Timothy of Tregairn
– Curtana Scarlet
Woman) 25.3.83.*

Thomas Fall

Ch Tudorhurst Tamora, as clever as she was beautiful, was a marvellous brood and showgirl, a daughter of Thomasina and Castleray Buccaneer (a Gay Royal son). She produced two litters to Royal Captive which included English and USA Ch Tudorhurst Tuscan Prince, USA Ch Tudorhurst Trojan Prince, Australian Ch Tudorhurst Thetis, Australian Ch Tudorhurst Theseus, Ch Tudorhurst Treasure and Tudorhurst Tambourine. Rebellion and Tambourine produced Ch Tudorhurst Royal Tribute, French Ch Tudorhurst Royal Tristram, Ch Tudorhurst Royal Theodora and Tudorhurst Royal Temptress. Another Royal Captive son was Australian Ch Tudorhurst Maximilian. Tambourine and Maplehurst Timothy of Tregairn produced Tudorhurst Taffeta and Ch Tudorhurst Tamarix. Taffeta mated to Morning Glory has produced French Ch Tudorhurst Magic Charm, USA Ch Tudorhurst Tapestry, Tudorhurst Tamsinastar, a winner of two challenge certificates, and Tudorhurst Truly Sweet. Ch Tudorhurst Tamarix, in her first litter of six to Ch Graslon Adonis of Zepherine, produced Tudorhurst Trouble, winner of one challenge certificate, and to Ch Zepherine Pierrot of Marbanks she has again had six puppies. Tudorhurst Theron and Tudorhurst Truly Fair were kept at home. Another daughter of Royal Temptress was Ch Tudorhurst Rosalinda; the sire was Maplehurst Timothy of Tregairn.

Sambo of Zubaida, Pauline Sharp's tenth birthday present to my daughter Julia, started the Curtanas. Sambo's daughter, Jessica of Tudorhurst, was mated to Simon and produced Julia's first Champion – Ch Tudorhurst Sir Lionel. Zepherine Beaucaire, a small mis-marked ruby, a gift from Mrs Birchall to Julia, was mated to Jessica. The result was the legendary Ch Curtana Morgana and her litter sister Curtana Guinevere. Guinevere and Royal Captive produced Curtana Scarlet Woman, who produced Ch Curtana Legend and Ch Curtana Lynette, following a mating to Maplehurst Timothy of Tregairn. Just once in a lifetime do you have that special relationship with a dog like Morgana. In her thirteen years of life she gave so much love and fun to Julia and the rest of the family. For her, shows were always fun, her tail never stopped wagging; her personality as well as her looks helped her to be the top winning King Charles Spaniel of all time with thirty-three challenge certificates. She will always be remembered for her sheer exuberance and joy of life.

In the Sixties Madeline Harper founded her Huntglen kennel. She purchased her stock mainly from Mrs Loader of the Leefland prefix. Her first home-bred champion was the black and tan Ch Huntglen Black Narcissus. She was born in 1967 and gained her title in 1970. She was sired by Atom of Leefland and was out of Huntglen Scarlet Pimpernel. Mrs

Julia Huggins' Ch Tudorhurst Sir Lionel (Ch Tudorhurst Simon – Jessica of Tudorhurst) 4.7.75.

Julia Huggins' Ch Curtana Morgana (Zepherine Beaucaire – Jessica of Tudorhurst) 26.3.76.

Thomas Fall

Julia Huggins' Ch Grenajay Julie's Boy of Curtana (Grenajay Joshua – Ch Jaynagret Lucinda) 7.8.87. Bred by Mrs Sheila Taylor and Miss Natalie Taylor.

Thomas Fall

Castle obtained the young Blenheim dog, Huntglen Darcy, bred by Mrs Harper and sired by Mrs Castle's dog Ch Charlie's Rapture of Oakridges. In 1972 Huntglen Darcy became a champion. The following year Mrs Harper purchased from Mrs Arkle-Smith the bitch destined to become Ch Huntglen April Jest. She also purchased Huntglen Southwardedge Priscilla from Mrs Doris Horton and this dog gained her title in 1974. From her whole colour line Mrs Harper bred Ch Huntglen Black Adam 1972, a name still evident in some of the whole colours being shown today.

With the advent of Mrs Birchall's extensive breeding programme, many new adherents arrived in the breed. In 1969 Mr and Mrs Gordon Pedley obtained Zepherine Paulette and Zepherine Ottaline. Paulette, mated to Mrs Rita Evans' Spencer of Valevan, produced Moordown Dante, later to be Ch Moordown Dante of Valevan. Spencer of Valevan was a Gay Royal grandson. Litter sister to Dante was Moordown Minerva, who was purchased by Mrs Fry and, when mated to Ch Corosco Peerless Peter, produced Ch Amantra Only Agnes. Another daughter of Paulette's and Spencer's was Moordown Dolly Girl, who, mated to a Zepherine Sanatra son, produced Mr Stumpy of Valevan.

Mr and Mrs Pedley purchased Dorsyl Sophie from Mr Lloyd and Mrs Cooper. Sophie was mated to Mr Stumpy of Valevan and produced

THE KING CHARLES IN THE 20TH CENTURY

Moordown Sasha, a cornerstone of the Moordown breeding. Sasha mated to Sanatra produced Ch Moordown Chequered Skipper and also Song of Zepherine for Mrs Birchall. When Sasha was mated to Charpoint Valentino of Valevan (a son of Sanatra), she produced Ch Moordown Morning Glory of Tudorhurst. In 1970 Mr and Mrs Frank Coupe started to exhibit. They obtained a tri-colour bitch from Mrs Birchall, Zepherine Leila, a daughter of Zepherine Lupin of Pantisa. In 1974 Leila and Zepherine Adair produced Marbanks Marius and Marbanks Mariella. Later the Coupes obtained the outstanding tri-colour Ch Zepherine Pierrot of Marbanks and his brother Zepherine Beau Geste. When Mrs Birchall died, Zepherine Juniper spent his remaining days with Mr and Mrs Coupe and his sons. Graslon Belair of Zepherine also lives with them. Ch Zepherine Pierrot of Marbanks, along with the other dogs left by Mrs Birchall, have made their mark on the breed, as so many others have done before them.

In 1974 Mrs Robins obtained Zepherine Hairbelle from Mrs Birchall, and the Maplehursts had arrived. In 1979 Ch Maplehurst Romeo was born, a truly lovely Blenheim, very sound, with a melting expression. He was campaigned in the ownership of both Mrs Joyce Robins and Mrs Sheila Waters of the Maibee kennels, where he ended his days. Mrs Robins was also the breeder of Ch Maplehurst Violetta, a Zepherine Hairbelle granddaughter and Zepherine Sanatra daughter. She was owned by Mrs Val Stringer. Mrs Soper Dyer obtained Maplehurst Serina of Tregairn from Mrs Robins, and, when mated to Maplehurst Jamie, she produced Ch Tregairn Rebecca for Mrs Sheila Taylor of the Jaynagret King Charles. Rebecca was mated to Ch Maplehurst Romeo and produced the two winning dogs Jaynagret Ryan and Jaynagret Roscoe. When Rebecca was mated to Grenajay Beau Olly she produced the outstanding tri-colour champion Jaynagret Nathaniel and his full sister Ch Jaynagret Lucinda. Lucinda in her litter to Grenajay Joshua, a grandson of Jaynagret Ryan, has produced Grenajay Julie's Boy of Curtana, a tri-colour with two challenge certificates, and Grenajay Adam, a Blenheim. Using Mrs Robins' and Mrs Waters' Ch Larkrise Red Robin, Mrs Taylor has produced the outstanding young ruby dog, Jaynagret Zachary. Mrs Taylor is a breeder who puts her knowledge and experience to good use.

Eddie and Barbara Plews owe their foundations to Mrs Robins with Maplehurst Annette. She was the dam of their Ch Teewhit Just William, and bred some marvellous puppies for them. Barry and Sheila Byers also own two Maplehurst champions, Ch Maplehurst Simeon, a black and tan son of Mrs Waters' and Mrs Robins' Ch Larkrise Red Robin, and Ch

Mr and Mrs Frank Coupe's Ch Zepherine Pierrot of Marbanks bred by Mrs Joyce Birchall (Zepherine Juniper – Song of Zepherine) 30.9.82.

Maplehurst Anneka, a tri-colour. Ch Simmanie Corny's Pride, a Blenheim, was sired by Maplehurst Cornelius, the dam being Maplehurst Antigone. From Anneka and Ch Graslon Adonis came Ch Simmaine Annalise.

In 1973 Mrs Rita Evans' tri-colour dog, Winston Evans of Maxholt, which she had purchased from Mrs Peggy Talbot in 1969, became a champion. Bitten by the bug of showing and exhibiting, the Valevans were on the way. By 1977 Ch Winston Evans of Maxholt's grandson, Moordown Dante of Valevan, was a champion. Ch Valevan Gwilliam Sir William, a son of Mr Stumpy of Valevan, followed. From Mrs Sally Charman, Mrs Evans purchased Ch Charpoint Snow Crystal of Valevan, a lovely tri-colour bitch.

In the mid-Seventies, Mrs Diane Fry began to breed and exhibit her Amantra King Charles. Her first champion was Ch Amantra Only Agnes, a daughter of Moordown Minerva and Ch Corosco Peerless Peter. Her

Tudorhurst Tamsinastar (Ch Moordown Morning Glory of Tudorhurst – Tudorhurst Taffeta) 14.2.87.
Thomas Fall

Mr and Mrs Frank Coupe's Graslon Belair of Zepherine bred by Roy Davies (Zepherine Chorister – Zepherine Claudine) 10.9.83.

Joyce Robin's Ch Maplehurst Romeo owned by Mrs Sheelagh Waters (Zepherine Nicholas – Maplehurst Julietta). Panther Photographics

next was Ch Eastonite Summers Day at Amantra, a Blenheim bred by Mrs Ellis and sired by Mrs Cooper's Ch Dorsyl Red Pepper. Then followed Ch Amantra Woody Nightshade, a tri-colour, and Ch Amantra Chameleon, another son of Ch Dorsyl Red Pepper, an outstanding Blenheim who did much to further the breed. After him, came Ch Amantra Othello and Ch Love Affair at Amantra.

From Mrs Fry, Mrs Brenda Essex obtained Amantra My Domino, and from Mrs Parry came Glenhurst Abba and Glenhurst Golden Michael. In 1981 Michael achieved his title to become Ch Glenhurst Golden Michael of Brendek. His son, the outstanding ruby Brendek Golden Wonder, is now ten-and-a-half years old and is still winning today. The kindness of Mrs Essex has helped many breeders on the road to success. Ch Brendek Dorothea, a Blenheim owned by Malcolm and Carol Baldwin, is one example of her generosity, and so is Mrs Maureen Newman's Brendek Daysee, a glamorous tri-colour.

With the death of Mrs Birchall, Brian Rix and Kevin Berry received Graslon Adonis of Zepherine, litter brother to Roy Davies' beautiful bitch, Ch Graslon Aphrodite. Adonis, along with the bitch Zepherine Belle Brocade who was also left to Mr Berry and Mr Rix, both quickly gained their titles. A litter from Belle Brocade and Zepherine Juniper produced the homebred champion Ch Ricksbury Annabelle, and Belle Brocade's litter by Ch Graslon Adonis produced Ch Ricksbury Aramis.

The increased interest shown by so many in breeding and exhibiting King Charles, particularly by those experienced and established in other breeds, looks promising for the future, and the enthusiasm of the newcomers will do much to promote and perpetuate this lovely breed. Mrs Ann Wynyard of the Braeduke Tibetan Spaniels bred some lovely whole colours in the past; the ruby Braeduke Red Primrose appears in pedigrees today. Recently we have been joined by some of the leading Cavalier breeders. Mrs Caroline Gillies (McGoogans) owned King Charles over twenty years ago, along with Mrs Barbara Keswick (Pargeter), Mrs Daphne Murray (Crustadele) and Mrs Sheila Halsall (Pantisa), all names of the past. Mrs Gillis has since renewed her interest, along with Mrs Diana Schlizzi (Chacombe), Mrs Lorraine Higgins (Cottismeer) who bred Ch Cottismeer Candi of Dicarl, and Mrs Joan Winters (Kentonville). Alan Hall and John Evans (Alansmere) have always had a King Charles Spaniel. Ricksbury (Rix and berry), Maibee (Mrs S. Waters), Oakmill (Barker & Briggs) and Kirklyn (Mrs Lyndesay-Smith) have had winning dogs in both breeds.

Mrs Diane Fry's Ch Amantra Othello (Amantra Wild Arum – Amantra The Muppet from Saldawn) 10.7.82.

Mrs Diane Fry's Ch Amantra Chameleon (Ch Dorsyl Pepper – Amantra Mayweed) 10.12.80.

Thomas Fall

Mrs Brenda Essex's Brendek Golden Wonder (Ch Glenhurst Golden Michael of Brendek – Amantra Midnight Melody) 23.5.79.   Panther Photographics

Ch Maplehurst Simeon (Ch Larkrise Red Robin – Maplehurst Emily) 21.12.82. Breeder: Mrs Joyce Robins. Owners: Mr & Mrs Barry Byers.

Mrs Diane Fry's Ch Amantra Only Agnes (Ch Corosco Peerless Peter of Oakridges – Moordown Minerva) 28.10.79.

Thomas Fall

CHAPTER FOUR

Breed Standard of the Cavalier King Charles Spaniel

General appearance: Active, graceful and well balanced, with gentle expression.

Characteristics: Sporting, affectionate, absolutely fearless.

Temperament: Gay, friendly, non-aggressive; no tendency to nervousness.

Head and skull: Skull almost flat between ears. Stop shallow. Length from base of stop to tip of nose about 1½ inches. Nostrils black and well developed without flesh marks, muzzle well tapered. Lips well developed but not pendulous. Face well filled below eyes. Any tendency to snipiness undesirable.

Eyes: Large, dark, round but not prominent; spaced well apart.

Ears: Long, set high, with plenty of feather.

Mouth: Jaws strong, with a perfect, regular and complete scissor bite, i.e. the upper teeth closely overlapping the lower teeth and set square to the jaws.

Neck: Moderate length, slightly arched.

Forequarters: Chest moderate, shoulders well laid back; straight legs moderately boned.

Body: Short-coupled with good spring of rib. Level back.

Hindquarters: Legs with moderate bone; well turned stifle – no tendency to cow or sickle hocks.

Ch Dickon of Little Breach, illustrating the ideal requirements of the breed standard.

Thomas Fall

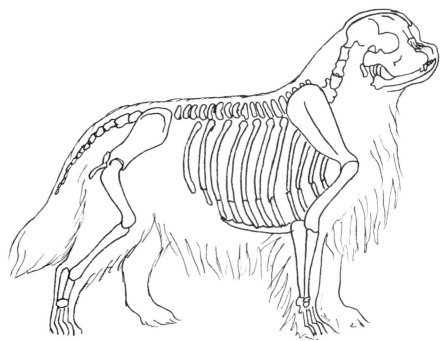

Skeletal outline of the Cavalier.

Feet: Compact, cushioned and well feathered.

Tail: Length of tail in balance with body, well set on, carried happily but never much above the level of the back. Docking optional. If docked no more than one-third to be removed.

Gait/Movement: Free moving and elegant in action, plenty of drive from behind. Fore and hind legs move parallel when viewed from in front and behind.

Coat: Long, silky, free from curl. Sight wave permissible. Plenty of feathering. Totally free from trimming.

Colour: Recognised colours are:
Black and Tan: Raven black with tan markings above the eyes, on cheeks, inside ears, on chest and legs and underside of tail. Tan should be bright. White marks undesirable.
Ruby: Whole coloured rich red. White markings undesirable.
Blenheim: Rich chestnut markings well broken up, on pearly white ground. Markings evenly divided on head, leaving room between ears for much valued lozenge mark or spot (a unique characteristic of the breed).
Tricolour: Black and white well spaced, broken up, with tan markings over eyes, cheeks, inside ears, inside legs, and on underside of tail.
Any other colour or combination of colours most undesirable.

Size: Weight: 12-18 pounds. A small well-balanced dog well within these weights desirable.

Faults: Any departure from the foregoing points should be considered a fault and the seriousness with which the fault should be regarded should be in exact proportion to its degree.

Note: Male animals should have two apparently normal testicles fully descended into the scrotum.

The Standard of the Cavalier as laid down by the Kennel Club on the advice of the combined Cavalier clubs stresses the dog's delightful, sweet nature, and any Cavalier that does not fulfil these requirements would be entirely foreign to the breed. The breed has all the attributes of the ideal family pet; it is easy-going and not as strong-willed as the King Charles,

The perfect head. Ch Crisdig Leading Seaman.

Head Studies.

considering everyone a friend, while the King Charles is more a connoisseur in his choice of friends.

The head of the Cavalier is one of the focal points of the breed. The expression must be sweet and gentle with a soft, full muzzle without any hint of coarseness or snipiness. The standard states that the stop should be shallow but I find this a little misleading. The most desirable heads have a moderate stop; a shallow stop gives a rather bland, mean expression and loses the soft fullness. The correct length of nose to balance the flat skull is required. If it is too short the dog becomes reminiscent of a first-cross King Charles; if it is too long, there is a resemblance to a Welsh Springer. The eyes should be dark and round, but not so large as to appear prominent. They should certainly show no white of eye or be so small or close-set as to give a mean expression. The same applies to light eyes, which are extremely difficult to breed out. Some Cavaliers suffer from blocked tear ducts which causes the eyes to weep constantly, and subsequently brown stains appear. Another cause of staining can be entropion, which is excessive flow of tears caused by eyelashes on both or either lower and upper lids turning into the eyeball and causing intense irritation. Both these faults are hereditary. The Standard on mouth

Jawlines: Cavalier

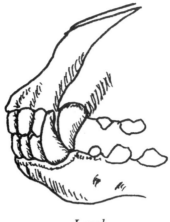

Level

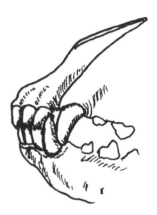

Scissor, seen from the side.

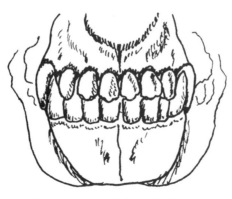

Scissor, viewed from the front.

requirements has changed from "level bite" to "level bite but scissor bite preferred", and finally "regular, complete scissor bite". Mouths can be a problem, not surprisingly as the King Charles requires an under-shot jaw. Some Cavalier youngsters appear to go wrong with the change of teeth but many mouths rectify to a perfect scissor by fifteen months.

A Cavalier with a neck of moderate length, and slightly arched and with good shoulder placement, moves with pride and elegance. Two great dogs of the past, Ch Pargeter McBounce and Ch Dickon of Little Breach, illustrate the ideal outline, proud and assured. A short neck and straight shoulder makes a Cavalier appear stuffy and coarse: often this type of dog may win as a youngster but as the pup reaches maturity the fault becomes more obvious and unattractive.

The Cavalier Standard calls for a short-coupled animal with good spring of rib. In comparison the King Charles is more barrel-chested, wider and deeper. The fronts and hindquarters of both the King Charles and Cavaliers are similar, possibly the King Charles' fronts have more width, due to the greater spring of rib required. A Cavalier that is narrow behind will often have long hocks, always carry its tail incorrectly and is usually cow-hocked. Luxating patellas cause the same problem in both breeds. A bad top-line, often so apparent in the breed, completely spoils both outline and movement. The old Cavalier Standard, like that of the King Charles, appeared to ignore movement, and it is a credit to the older breeders that they always laid stress on the fact that a Cavalier should be sporting and sound. This is a legacy that all future breeders should hold dear. The graceful contours of the outline of the Cavalier when standing should not be lost once the dog is required to move.

The ideal coat is flat, profuse and silky; a curly coat is not only the wrong texture, it also tends to spoil the outline of the dog. As with King Charles Spaniels, the richness of the colours is one of the beauties of the Cavalier. A few years back there was a move among some breeders to accept the black and black-and-white Cavaliers that appeared from time to time. They felt that the black toy spaniel depicted by Mignard in his painting of the Dauphin (Louis XV) had a true Cavalier head, ears and eyes, and was very typical. Although these two colours appear in Cavalier breeding, the majority of breeders felt the colours were not acceptable and the proposition was rejected.

Size has always been very much a matter of personal choice. Balance and symmetry is more important than actual weight. Probably very few Cavaliers (or King Charles Spaniels) are actually within their stipulated weight limits of 12-18 lbs, but it is important to bear this in mind, although bone and substance must not be lost at any price.

Hound Type.

Undershot.

Too domed, deep stop.

Face too short, showing white of eye.

Too snipey.

No stop.

Small piggy eyes.

Correct.

Cavalier pacing: An ugly and incorrect movement as the body tends to roll along as the dog shifts its weight from side to side.

Correct topline and tail carriage.

Incorrect.

CHAPTER FIVE

The Cavalier 1926–1989

THE following announcement appeared in the catalogue of Charles Cruft's 1926 Dog Show:

'Blenheim Spaniels of the Old Type, as shown in pictures of Charles II's time, long face, no stop, flat skull not inclined to be domed, with a spot in centre of skull. The first prizes in classes 947 and 948 are given by Roswell Eldridge Esq., of New York, and will be continued for five years. Prizes go to the nearest to type required.'

The £25 offered by Mr Roswell Eldridge would have been a considerable fortune nearly seventy years ago. The feather boas in the King Charles Spaniel Club must have quivered in outrage! The following extract from *Dog World*, January 18, 1929 written by Mrs Harold Budge, gives some insight into the depth of feeling:

'I have been asked what is a Cavalier King Charles. It is the name which has been given to the long-faced King Charles in an effort to bring back and standardise the old type of Spaniel. I believe there have been several attempts made in the past, but most of them have been doomed to failure, and the present phase dates back to Cruft's 1926, when the late Mr Roswell Eldridge, of New York, offered two prizes of £25 each for the best Blenheim dog and bitch approximating to the old type. I shall never forget the storm that was raised about dogs, that would not be eligible for a prize in a King Charles class on looks, being able to walk away with £25 for being a bad King Charles.

'In those days they were described by Mr Whiting as "Yiddisher King Charles", whilst another fancier, almost the grandfather of the breed, informed us he had drowned all his eligibles as puppies. Because of this bubble my husband tried to get the Club to petition the Kennel Club to separate the "nosey from the noseless", but everyone was so certain that it would fizzle out that nothing was done. They reckoned without Mrs Hewitt Pitt, who has taken up the matter with such vigour that there is now a Cavalier King Charles Spaniel Club, with a separate standard recognised by the Kennel Club, and with nine classes on at Crufts, including the two twenty-five pounders. These are being judged by Mr Frank Butler.'

On February 15, 1929, after Cruft's, Mrs Budge wrote:

'After what I have written recently about the Cavaliers, I was naturally

*Sw Ch Kingmaker
of Ttiweh and Ch
Oyster Pattie of
Ttiweh at Dumfries
1961. Judge Miss
Pamela Turle.*
M. Cook & Son

*Cavalier King
Charles belonging to
Madame J. Harper
des-Trois Fontains,
1939.*

Thomas Fall

*interested in them so I took a walk round their benches as soon as I arrived at the
show. I was rather intrigued at first by the diversity of type, but when I realised
that the judge had to pick out two of these dogs and make them a present of £25
each, I was struck by the job which confronted the judge. The next step was to
find Mr Frank Butler, whom I asked what he intended judging on and if he had
the Cavalier Club standard. He very kindly showed me some old engravings he
had obtained of the actual Stuart family with their dogs and said that was the
type he was going for. I must say Mr Butler judged conscientiously, according to
the type he required, and although some of the classes looked like a variety class,
it was always possible to follow the awards from the ringside.*

'*Miss Mostyn-Walker won the £25 for dogs with a Blenheim called Ann's
Son, a rather taking dog and not unlike a Welsh Cocker. Mrs Raymond
Mallock won the £25 for bitches with Ashton-More Flora. I should like to say
that Flora was, in my opinion, the best-coated and conditioned King Charles in
the show of any type, and stood out in this class. Mrs Hewitt Pitt, Miss
Sparrow, Mrs Whyte, Mrs Higgs, Mrs Fielding and Mrs Hammond were all
in the money in these classes, while Mrs Hewitt-Pitt won both Brace and Team.
The exhibitors turned up in good numbers. All the classes were well filled, and
they took the awards in a very sporting manner, a lesson that could well be learnt
in other rings. Also they had not made a fetish of colour; consequently they have
the whole of the fancy to breed from.*'

Ann's Son was a very beautiful little dog and he captured the hearts and
imaginations of the early breeders – both Cavalier and King Charles. Mrs
Phylis Watson of the Aviemore King Charles and Mrs Mabel Gristwood of
the St Lucia King Charles were great admirers of the dog and remember
him well: fine-muzzled, flat-skulled, lovely dark eyes and beautiful long
ears, he weighed about ten to twelve pounds.

Mrs Pitt wrote: '*. . . a small Blenheim dog, bred out of a short-faced
bitch, probably by a Papillon sire. He was probably the best ever, as he really
was a Toy Dog. Unfortunately, although his owner tried hard to repeat this dog,
her efforts were not successful and she turned her attention to breeding pocket
Cockers.*'

The breeding of Ann's Son was endorsed by Mr Percy Holmes of the
Noranor King Charles and a great friend of Miss Mostyn Walker and by
Mrs Whiting of the Minaster King Charles, who stated: '*Ann's Son was the
offspring of a tri-colour bitch and a Papillon.*'

Wizbang Timothy, brother to Ann's Son, was not as attractive, and he
was nearly a black and white; but he was an excellent stud dog.
Unfortunately the poor dog seems to have had a rather unhappy life as he
moved through various homes, contracting sarcoptic mange and was
invariably in poor condition. There is not a Cavalier in the country who

Ch Minshang Corinna (The Young Pretender of Greenwich – Annabelle of Astondowns) Mar '46. Breeder: Mrs H. Pilkington. Owner: Mrs Joyce Green.

Thomas Fall

Ch Minshang Sir Roger (Ch Daywell Roger – Mingshang Sarah) Aug '47. Owner-breeder: Miss P. Mayhew.

Thomas Fall

does not go back to Ann's Son and his brother in some marked degree.

According to Mrs Gristwood, Mrs Raymond Mallock's Ashtonmore Flora was no good as a brood having been sent on breeding terms to Mrs Beeching at Maidstone. But she was bought back later to win the prize. Flora weighed about fifteen pounds and had heavy chestnut markings, good flat skull and was sound. She was sold for £7 in 1930.

Only a breeder with determination, dedication and an in-depth knowledge of genetics would embark on the challenge the new breed presented, and Mrs Amice Pitt had all the qualities required. She had inherited from her father, Sir Everett Millais, himself a noted dog breeder and geneticist, her love of dogs and appreciation of his scientific approach to dog breeding. In 1928 the Cavalier King Charles Spaniel Club was formed, a toss of the coin deciding the positions of Miss Mostyn Walker as chairman and Mrs Pitt as secretary. With her daughter Jane, now Mrs Bowdler, Mrs Pitt showed teams of Cavaliers up and down the country, gaining hard-won support for the breed. They proved to be great ambassadors as the ranks swelled and the following grew, only to be shattered by the outbreak of war in 1939. From a kennel of sixty Cavaliers and twenty Chows, Mrs Pitt and Jane kept only three Cavaliers and two Chows.

As with the King Charles breeders, who emerged with a small nucleus of dogs, Mrs Pitt wrote 'After the war there was no choice for a breeding plan and the only possible course was to jump back to the source and get as near to Ann's Son as possible.'

The January of 1945 was another milestone in Cavalier history, when the Kennel Club granted a separate register for Cavalier Spaniels; and in 1946 the Cavalier King Charles Spaniel Club held its first championship show. There were twenty-eight Cavaliers entered and Best in Show went to Mrs Katie Eldred's Belinda of Saxham, a Blenheim granddaughter of Ann's Son. Mrs Eldred was secretary of the Cavalier Club from 1945 to 1948 and owner of the Turnham Cavaliers, who for some time have been resident in Canada. Her sister was Mrs Daphne Murray who owned the Crustadele Cavaliers and King Charles. Mrs Eldred also bred Mrs Pitt's Ch Little Dorrit of Ttiweh from her Belinda sired by Bouncer Rupert, who was a tri-colour dog of Mrs Jennings' Plantation breeding.

The best dog at that momentous first championship show was Daywell Roger, who became the breed's first champion and leading stud dog of his era. Ch Daywell Roger and Ch Little Dorrit of Ttiweh produced Ch Harmony of Ttiweh, Ch Jupiter of Ttiweh and Mars of Ttiweh, the foundation sires for most of the present-day Cavaliers.

Mrs Harper des-Trois Fontaines, a Belgian by birth, was known mainly for her Pyrenean kennel. She was a formidable lady, with a reputation as a shrewd business woman. The prefix de Fontenay is behind many of the early Cavaliers, and is important in that Mrs Harper des Trois-Fontaines kept Cavaliers going through the perilous war period, although by the Fifties her interest in Cavaliers had waned. Two other very important breeders in the early years were Miss Phylis Mayhew, who was already an established and well-respected Pekingese breeder, with the prefix of Minshang, and her sister Mrs Joyce Green of the Heathersides. Both prefixes were well known for their small quality Cavaliers, well within the weights laid down by the standard, and many famous champions have appeared bearing the Mingshang and Heatherside prefix. Another interesting prefix that appears in both King Charles and Cavalier breeding is the 'of Grenewich'. Mrs Maud Sawkins was a rather absent-minded lady who had a black and tan King Charles, Rupert of Grenewich, who was used extensively to revive the flagging whole colours in King Charles after the war. Her Blenheim Cavalier dog, The Young Pretender of Grenewich, figures in many of the Cavalier pedigrees.

At the end of the Forties, Mrs Barbara Keswick acquired her first Cavaliers and the great Pargeter kennels were founded. Mrs Keswick will always be remembered for her kindness and generosity in both breeds. She required her Cavaliers to be sound with plenty of substance. Over the years, numerous Pargeters have acquired their titles both at home and abroad. Pargeter stock was used to found Cavalier kennels in the United States. Miss Elizabeth Spalding's Kilspindies being one of the most famous. In Australia, New Zealand and Sweden breeders have all benefited from Mrs Keswick's breeding and knowledge. The Irish-based Tnegun kennel of Mrs Amy Nugent is founded mainly on Ttiweh and Pargeter bloodlines, and over the years they have built their own very distinct type. Mrs Keswick's death in 1969 was felt by all who knew her, both in Cavaliers and King Charles. Ch Pargeter McBounce will be remembered as a model for the breed by many.

The Hillbarn Cavaliers of Mrs Helen Pilkington, famous for many lovely typical tri-colours, were campaigned extensively. After the death of Roger Pilkington, Mrs Barbara Percival took on her cousin's dogs and prefix, showing them in conjunction with her own already well known Little Breach kennels. Ch Dickon of Little Breach is still used as a model to illustrate the breed, nearly twenty-five years later. The Fifties were dominated by the Ttiwehs, Pargeters, Hillbarns, Minsghangs and the Heathersides, until 1956 when Miss Pamela Turle bred a grandson of Ch Daywell Roger. He was a tri-colour called Ch Aloysius of Sunninghill and he became the breed recordholder, with a tally of nineteen challenge

Ch Minshang Fabian (Ch Minshang Sir Roger – Minshang Rosalind) Nov '49. Owner-Breeder: Miss Phylis Mayhew.

Thomas Fall

Little Breach Cavaliers 1965.

Thomas Fall

*Mrs Helen
Pilkington with
some of the Hillbarn
Cavaliers, 1952.*

Thomas Fall

*Ch Unity of
Hillbarn (Ch
Hillbarn Desmond –
Renee of Hillbarn)
Jul '55.
Owner-breeder: Mrs
Helen Pilkington.*

Thomas Fall

certificates, and the sire of eight champions.

In 1958 Lady Forword campaigned Ch Infanta's Katherine of Eyeworth to her title; she was the first of many Eyeworth champions. Possibly the most famous was International Ch Pargeter McBounce's son Ch Archie McMuck of Eyeworth. In 1959, the Crisdigs, one of the most famous and far-reaching strains of Cavaliers, was established by Mrs Susan Burgess. Colonel and Mrs Burgess purchased the two half-sisters, Vairire Charmaine and Vairire Venetia from Mrs Burroughes. Charmaine gained her title in 1961 to become Ch Vairire Charmaine of Crisdig. Her dam Vairire Candida was out of a half-brother sister union, the common parent being Ch Daywell Roger. Charmaine was by a son of Ch Sunninghill Perseus of Lochfee, a Ch Aloysius son, and a Ch Raoul of Ttiweh grandson. Ch Raoul was also a Ch Daywell Roger grandson. Charmaine's half-sister Venetia was also a daughter of Vairire Candida, this time bred to Rudolph of Crustadele, a Ch Daywell Roger grandson through Ch Prologue of Ttiweh. When Vairire Venetia of Crisdig was put to Crisdig Henry, Charmaine's son by Pound Foolish of Ttiweh, and a very potent and famous stud dog, Ch Crisdig Celebration was born, along with his litter sisters Ch Crisdig Charm and Ch Crisdig Candid. A Celebration grandson, Ch Crisdig Leading Seaman, has with his impeccable breeding become a potent stud force in his own right. Few breeders can have made such an impact over so many years and this has continued with the more recent champions: Ch Crisdig Ted, Ch Crisdig Cracker, Ch Crisdig Robinson, Ch Crisdig Marion, Ch Crisdig Girl Friday and Ch Crisdig Angelique. Many famous kennels have laid their foundations on Crisdig stock, including Mrs and Miss Boardman's Ch Crisdig Peace of Volney.

Mrs Burroughes' Vairire kennel housed both Cavaliers and King Charles Spaniels. In fact, Ch Vairire Osiris and Ch Vairire Duchess Xenia of Santander were out of a ruby, Vairire Isis, a granddaughter of Zepherine Torquil's Rose. Torquil's Rose was a Cavalier, originally owned by Joyce Birchall and then passed on to Mrs Burroughes. Ch Vairire Osiris sired Ch Rosemullion of Ottermouth and Ch Rose Mary of Ottermouth for Mrs Gertrude Biddle. Ch Rosemullion was an important stud force with impeccable breeding, and when his sister Rose Mary was put to Ch Crisdig Harlequin, she produced Ch Ottermouth Back Badge.

Mrs Caroline Gillies' kennel of McGoogans Cavaliers came to the fore during the mid-Sixties when she bred Ch McGoogans Ruari, a Blenheim, by Crisdig Jaspar out of a Ch Aloysius of Sunninghill daughter. A very lovely Blenheim daughter of Ruari was sold to Alan Hall and John Evans and became Ch Alansmere McGoogans Maggie May. They had previously

Ch Bowstones Victoria of Little Breach (Ch Barings Fortescue — Bowstones Piprage) Apr '62. Breeder: Mrs I. Booth. Owner: Mrs Barbara Percival.

Thomas Fall

Mrs Susan Burgess and Crisdig Celebration at Bath 1964, judge Miss Pamela Turle and Miss Betty Miller with Ch Otterholt Cold Cream.

M. Cooke & Son

Ch Crisdig Merry Matelot (Ch Crisdig Celebration – Ch Vairire Charmaine of Crisdig) Dec '64. Owner-breeder: Mrs Susan Burgess.

Thomas Fall

purchased a Blenheim daughter of Ch Crisdig Celebration, McGoogans Molly Malone. In 1973, their dog Alansmere Aquarius made history by going Best in Show at Crufts. His dam was Ch Alansmere McGoogans Maggie May who was sired by Ch Vairire Osiris. Such an outstanding achievement is hard to follow but the Alansmeres went from strength to strength. Aquarius' great grandson, the stylish Ch Alansmere Sandmartin, proved his worth in the late Seventies, producing a number of champions including Ch Alansmere Rosetta of Crieda and Ch Alansmere Michelle. Michelle has proved to be an excellent brood and the dam of many top class winners, notably Ch Alansmere Rhett Butler now in the USA. Alansmere Fionna Harvey, an outstanding brood bitch, was put to Ch Homaranne Andy Capp, by Mr Hall and Mr Evans, and produced Ch Sweet Seraphim of Amantra for Mrs Diane Fry.

A repeat of the 1975 litter in 1976, this time in the ownership of Mrs Diane Fry, produced Ch Amantra Bohemian Rhapsody. In 1977 Fionna Harvey was put to Amantra Petty Officer and gave Mrs Diane Fry and her daughter Tracey, Ch Amantra Anchors Away. Before Bohemian Rhapsody left for Australia he sired a son, Ch Amantra Roxy Music, and a daughter, Ch Amantra Bohemian Image. Bohemian Image put to Australian Ch Amantra Starboard produced Ch Amantra Pugwash.

One of the most respected breeders of Cavaliers and whole colours, with an incredible knowledge and memory for pedigrees, is Miss Molly Marshall of the Kormars. Ch Don Miguel of Kormar was a lovely black and tan, a grandson of Mrs Rennie's Ch Royalist of Veren on his sire's side, and on his dam's side a Ch Abelard of Ttiweh grandson. It was not always easy for Molly to spare the time to exhibit, and transport was always a problem. On one occasion in 1963 Molly, Mrs Eve Young with her greyhound Heathermaid, Mrs Marjorie Bunting of Norwich and Norfolk fame, and myself, hired a small bus to take us to Glasgow for the Scottish Kennel Club Show. We left at four in the afternoon, motorways being non-existent then, on a memorable journey. Our little bus sped north with an emergency driver who turned out to be a mechanic, who had never felt the desire to take a test. The first corner we took sent us sprawling on the floor. Our driver had decided to dispense with the seat fixtures to allow for room for his tools, petrol cans and oil. After all, Scotland was a foreign country to him, he had never been farther than Bedford, so he wanted to be prepared for all eventualities! Perched precariously on our seats we continued our journey with Heathermaid, the greyhound, standing sentinel the entire way to Glasgow and back. The only emergency rations our driver had not allowed for was water. Near to boiling as we chugged along, we used the dogs' water bowls filled from streams to refill the radiator. We arrived in Glasgow in time for judging. We all had a successful day and Don Miguel took his third and qualifying certificate under Leo Wilson. His black coat gleamed. Molly assured me that he had decided to honour the occasion by leaping into the bath with her just prior to leaving. He had arrived on the bus a little damp! We left Glasgow feeling elated, not knowing we were to embark on a sixteen-hour return journey. Our driver, probably in need of male camaraderie and liquid sustenance, stopped at a pub, where all the kind locals advised him on the best route to take home. The poor man became more and more confused; as a result more stops for liquid sustenance became necessary. Skipton, Ilkley and Otley are very attractive parts of the country, but our appetite for their beauty became a little jaded after revisiting them on countless occasions, arriving from different directions, all in one night.

Miss Marshall always favoured the small compact cavaliers and her Ruy Evanlgn of Kormar, a ruby, was just such a dog. When Mrs Diana Schlizzi combined Ruy Evanlyn with her Belle of Kormar, she produced the black and tan Ch Ivan the Terrible of Chacombe and the ruby Ch Cordelia of Chacombe. Belle of Kormar was a granddaughter of Ch Don Miguel. Cordelia, put to Mrs Ricketts' Ch Edgebourne Red Rake of Caplode, produced Ch Chacombe Camilla, the first ruby to win Best of Breed at Crufts in 1978. In 1970 Mrs Schlizzi had obtained from Mrs Barbara Percival a tri-colour puppy out of Ch Odette of Littlebreach, who was to become Ch Venetia of Littlebreach. When she was put to an impeccably bred Blenheim, Jamie of Littlebreach, she produced Ch Chacombe Alexis. Mrs Joan Winters, with her long-established Kentonvilles, used Ch Chacombe Alexis to produce Ch Kentonville Fern's Son. An earlier litter using Jamie of Littlebreach produced Ch Kentonville's Holly's Tansy. Ch Littlebreach Zachary of Chacombe, another son of Ch Alexis of Chacombe, produced Ch Rivermoor Lady Dorothy for Mr Michael and Miss Valerie Harvey, another well established and consistent kennel. Another successful breeder to base her Cavaliers on the Littlebreach lines is Mrs Leonie Wood with the Beamshaws. Ch Lance of Beamshaw and Ch Romulus of Beamshaw were both grandsons of Ch Dickon of Littlebreach.

One of the most prominent breeders since the early Seventies has been, without doubt, Mrs Molly Coaker with her daughter Anne – Homerbrent and Homeranne respectively. Crisdig was the firm base on which they built their bloodlines, and they have emerged as one of the most consistent kennels in the country today. The outstanding Ch Homeranne Caption has been Top Stud Dog since 1980, an unbeatable record in any breed. With an injection of new blood from Ireland, in the form of English and

Crufts 1973: Left Crisdig Florida and Mrs Susan Burgess, judge Mr V. Bennett and Alansmere Aquarius with John Evans.

M. Cooke & Son

Ch Stellers Eider of Pantisa. Owned by Mr and Mrs Duncan Gillies.

Pearce

Ch Amantra
Pugwash (left) and
Ch Amantra
Anchors Away.

Thomas Fall

Irish Champion Ronnoc Rhum of Sancem, the Coakers have continued their winning ways with Ch Heidi of Homerbrent, Ch Homeranne Carson, Ch Homerbrent Romeo, Ch Homerbrent Carnival, Ch Homerbrent Pentilly and Ch Homerbrent Festival, to name just a few from this kennel. One of the highlights must have been winning Best in Show with Ch Caroline of Homerbrent at the Diamond Jubilee Show, which celebrated sixty years of Cavaliers with a record seven hundred and seventy-eight exhibits.

Among the famous kennels who have based their breeding on Homerbrent bred stock are Mr and Mrs Inglis (Craigowl). Caption sired two notable champions, Craigowl Cashmere and Craigowl Storm of Homerbrent, for Mrs Inglis. Brian Rix and Kevin Berry (Ricksbury) had Ch Ricksbury Only Charm, another very lovely Blenheim daughter of Caption out of a homebred daughter of Crisdig breeding. Mrs Lorraine Higgins (Cottismeer) had Ch Cottismeer Gem Signet, a very beautiful Blenheim, this time by Homerbrent Samson. He was a Ch Tnegun Charivari son out of Ch Homerbrent Samantha. The dam of Gem Signet was Leynsord Velvet Glove of Cottismeer, herself a Ch Crisdig Leading Seaman daughter. All Cavaliers from this stock have been worthy ambassadors for their breed in all parts of the world.

A kennel with a meteoric rise to fame has been that of Miss Sheila Smith, breeding all four colours with great success. Basing her bloodlines on Pantisa of Mrs Sheila Halsall, she started with her Ch Salador Crystal Gayle, followed by such notable champions as Ch Salador Coppergleam, a ruby, the recordbreaking Ch Salador Celtic Prince, the youngest ever champion in the breed, and Ch Salador Crytalbelle, Ch Salador Crismark, Ch Salador Celtic Maid, Ch Salador Celtic Princess and Ch Salador Christo. After crossing the Irish seas to use Ronnoc True Luck, came Ch Salador Corrigan, Ch Salador Connors, and Ch Salador Colleen, all out of the same litter. In 1989 Ch Rheinvelt Ringold von Salador, a black and tan, took Best of Breed at Cruft's. The strong Salador stud team have been responsible for a large number of top winning dogs up and down the country as well as overseas.

East Anglia has produced some well known Cavalier kennels, one of the most famous being Mrs Pamela Thornhill with her Kindrums. Based originally on mainly Pargeter bloodlines, Mrs Thornhill has produced a line always recognisable for type. Ch Kindrum Sylvia was a multiple group winner, and a particularly beautiful representative of the breed. The latest Kindrum champion is Ch Kindrum Alberto, a grandson of Sylvia. America has been a great beneficiary of the Kindrum breeding, as

Ch Alansmere Rhett Butler (Alansmere Lamplighter – Ch Alansmere Michelle) March '83. Breeder: Messrs Hall & Evans. Owner: R. Calladine.

Thomas Fall

shown in the quality of the dogs now in the States. Many of the tri-colours shown today are the result of one lady's determined expertise, Mrs Peggy Talbot, who has remained undefeated by pain and disability. During the Seventies, Minstrel Boy of Maxholt was a prolific producer of tri-colours and was Top Stud Dog for two years, producing seven champions. One of his most famous sons was Ch Mintrode Jotham of Maxholt with twelve challenge certificates to his credit. The same breeding also produced Ch Mintrode Georgina of Maxholt. The line is continued today with great success by Mrs Virginia Barwell of the Charlottetown kennels. Ch Charlottetown Mackintosh carries all the selective breeding of the Maxholts.

During the past decade Cavaliers have continued to win group placements. Ch Jia Laertes of Tonnew, owned by Mr and Mrs Newton and bred by Mrs Dallas Archer, won the Toy Group at Cruft's in 1981. Ch Kindrum Alberto has just won the Toy Group Windsor 1989. Mrs Hewitt Pitt has left a heritage of which she would be inordinately proud. The show records speak for themselves, but it is the charming, happy personalities of the dogs that have been preserved by the dedicated breeders over the past sixty years, which would have given her the most pleasure.

Ch Chacombe Alexis (Jamie of Little Breach – Ch Venetia of Little Breach). Owner-breeder: Mrs Diana Schilizzi.

Thomas Fall

Ch Venetia of Little Breach and Ch Ivan The Terrible of Chacombe. Owner: Mrs Diana Schilizzi.

Thomas Fall

Homerbrent Champions: left to right: Caption, Carson, Carnival and Festival. Owner Mrs Molly Coaker.

Left: Ch Caroline of Homerbrent (Ch Homeranne Carson – Homerbrent Demelza).

Right: Ch Homerbrent Emerald (Ch Homaranne Caption – Ronnoc Solitaire of Homerbrent) Feb '84. Breeder: Mrs Molly Coaker. Owner: Mrs Thrupp.

Thomas Fall

Ch Homerbrent Samantha (Homerbrent Highlander – Homerbrent Annadrewan) Aug '72. Owner: Mrs Molly Coaker. Breeder: Mrs P. Mowe.

Thomas Fall

Ch Salador Celtic Maid (Ch Salador Celtic Prince – Ch Salador Coppergleam) Sept '82. Owner-breeder: Miss Sheila Smith.

Diane Pearce

Ch Salador Celtic Prince (Salador Chelsea of Loranka – Salador Cherrybird). Owner-breeder: Miss Sheila Smith.

Diane Pearce

Ch Salador Crystabelle and Ch Crystal Gayle. Owner-breeder: Miss Sheila Smith.

Dalton

Ch Salador Coppergleam (left) with her sire Salador Charlock. Owner-breeder: Miss Sheila Smith.

Dalton

Ch Charlottetown None So Fair (Charlottetown Inigo Jones – Fenella of Charlottetown) Oct '72. Owner-breeder: Mrs Virginia Barwell.

Ch Chamanic Lucasta (Sorata Llewellyn – Chamanic Bell Rock) Jan '86. Owner-breeder: Mrs A.J Inman.

Thomas Fall

CHAPTER SIX

English Toy Spaniels in America

IN the USA, the breed is known as English Toy Spaniel and has been recognised by the American Kennel Club since 1886. Originally called by colour designations – for example, Blenheim Spaniel and King Charles Spaniel – the name was changed near the turn of the century to ensure proper registration procedure as one breed, but divided into two varieties. These two varieties are still separated to this day and earn championship points in their separate classifications. Blenheim and Prince Charles are shown together, as are King Charles and Ruby, with the two representatives going into the toy group to compete with other breeds. In fact only recently have we seen both varieties take placings in the group finals.

The breed was very popular in the 1890s and the early years of this century, but started to lose ground to various other toy dogs through the Twenties and Thirties until it reached a low ebb of bare survival. After the Second World War several breeders began to achieve prominence and slowly started the breed on an upward climb. Names such as Celamo, Cedar Crest, Jekada, Veldale, Godric, Vica, Tarahall, Locksley Hall, Jaor and Clocroft became well known for typical, well-bred specimens. Through the Fifties and Sixties these names were joined by Brynmar, Suruca, Fotheringay, Luary, Harco and Doublejay. Starting in the Seventies and continuing to the present are Kingscourt Ebonwood Greenvale, Maranda, Nanda, Erins, Danaho, Amerglo, Thergay and Dreamridge. These have been joined more recently by Don-E-Brook, Little Pilgrim, Damelio and Kisn.

The breed's top winner was Ch Dreamridge Dear Charles, a King Charles dog bred by Susan Cain Jackson and owned by Thomas O'Neal. He achieved three all-breed championship best in shows, twenty toy groups, including such Stellar shows as Santa Barbara and Chicago International, and was certainly a great represenative of the breed, helping to further interest through his charming personality and showmanship.

The parent club, the English Toy Spaniel Club in America, currently has over sixty members and holds a highly successful annual breed speciality show each year. The breed is more numerous at shows and is becoming more successful with each year. There is no great desire to increase in huge numbers, as breed popularity can become a problem; but a stable population established in several areas of the USA will ensure continuation and appreciation of the English Toy Spaniel.

Ron Fabis

English and American Ch Tudorhurst Tuscan Prince.

Thomas Fall

JUDGING KING CHARLES SPANIELS
The first time I visited the United States of America to judge was in 1981. It was at the All Breeds Skokie Valley Show, the day prior to the first English Toy Spaniel Speciality Show to be judged by Mrs James Edward Clark. This was followed by a very well attended seminar chaired by Ron Fabis. We discussed the breed standard, how to pick puppies and how to prepare dogs for the show ring. My co-panellist on this occasion was Susan Cain Jackson of the wonderfully consistent Suruca whole colours.

At Skokie Valley I had no hesitation in awarding Susie's Ch Suruca Coreen Best of Breed; in any country she was an outstanding black and tan King Charles. Coreen's litter brother was the magnificent Ch Dreamridge

Dear Charles – a truly wonderful dog who won both Toy Groups and the final accolade of a Best in Show at the All Breeds Championship Show. Sadly his meteoric show career was cut short by a mystery virus, from which he never fully recovered. The sire of this lovely pair was Ch Harco's Towncrier, an ultra sound black and tan, who in spite of having injured his eye the previous day, strode round the ring to win Best in Show under Mrs Clark, at the time he was approaching his ninth birthday. His daughter Coreen took the Best Opposite Sex award. On my last visit to the States in 1986 Susie Cain Jackson had another beautiful black and tan in tow, Ch Suruca's Night Train, again perfectly constructed with a lovely head and well filled face, full of personality and character and quite a handful to show. Generally, the American whole colours are somewhat larger than the British counterparts, but we could certainly do with their construction and bone.

The Best of Variety in the broken colour under Mrs Clark was Mr T.F. O'Neal's Ch Tudorhurst Trojan Prince. He was also the sire of the winner's dog Ebonwood Shiloh O'Forest Glen owned by Mike Ossman, the winner of the puppy bitch class Thomas Kilcullen's Ebonwood Kiss Me In The Rain and the winner's bitch Thomas O'Neal's Dreamridge Dear Me, who later went Best Opposite Sex to the Best of Breed Winner. Needless to say, Ch Tudorhurst Trojan Prince won the Best Stud Dog award.

Five years later, it was very interesting to see the progress the breed had made. Some credit must go to Thomas O'Neal and Ron Fabis, who allow their beautiful home at Stonewalk to be used as a centre to foster the breed. Their hospitality and generosity have done so much to advance the interest in King Charles. The breeders are a wonderful warm and generous group who are quite prepared to travel from points as far-flung as California, Florida and Colorado to support their chosen breed.

My Best in Show was a really lovely Blenheim, Ch Dreamridge Dear Jeffrey, a great grandson of my much loved Ch Tudorhurst Tamora. A young tri-colour puppy of just six months caught my eye, a grandson of Ch Ebonwood Kiss Me In The Rain, who I had fallen in love with five years earlier. This young pup is Ch Dreamridge Dear Buzz, who had barnstormed his way round the States winning groups. The winner's dog was a well-made and heavy-boned dog of medium size, Fotheringay Patrick Golightly, bred by Richard Thomas and owned by Terence Childs and Karen Abbot Henderson. Terence Childs, along with Joseph R. Dhampagne, owned the winner's dog in the whole colour, a ruby called Fotheringay The Golightly, once again bred by Richard Thomas. Both dogs were sired by Ch Wildboy Bret of Eastfield. The winning bitch in the broken

colour was the very pretty and lovely mover, Wyemede's Crowning Glory, a tri-colour bred and owned by the Misses Julia and Elizabeth Crawford. She was sired by a dog from Florida called Ch Clancy of Double Jay, a tri-colour who has sired some lovely stock as well as being a considerable winner in his own right. Best Opposite Sex was an enchanting little baggage who was convinced Stonewalk had laid on a party for her benefit. The next day she appeared again at the Chain O'Lakes Show. I could hardly recognise the regal and perfectly behaved Ch Dreamridge Dark Eyes as the rascal of the day before. How she stood still long enough to be photographed, I will never know.

I was delighted to see Sheila Waters export Ch Kirklyn Jeeves of Maibee, a lovely son of Ch Maplehurst Romeo, one of my personal pin-up boys, bred by Mrs Margaret Lindesay-Smith. Originally, Jeeves went out to Mr Thomas Conway, but was bought by Christine Thaxton of the Kings Court King Charles. Christine is the breeder of the ruby, Ch Dreambridge Dragon of Kings Court, a very well-boned solid ruby who has sired many winners for both the Dreamridge and Kings Court Kennels. Christine also owns one of the prettiest small rubies I have seen, aptly named Rosebud. Another exhibitor who specialises in whole colours with considerable success is Susan Kisielewski. Many will remember her when she visited England for the King Charles Centenary.

One of the dearest visitors to our shows is Mary Hoagland. Every year she sportingly makes the long trip from New Jersey to Illinois to show her much-loved King Charles. Mary has had some beautiful King Charles over the years – Ch Luary Merissa, Ch Luary Nicola and Ch Luary Vulcan – to name just a few of her many homebred champions.

As in England most of the King Charles are owner-handled; the naughty but delightful temperament of the breed does not make them suitable subjects for the professional handler. They are a breed that is too personal in outlook and too devoted to their owners to adapt to the rigours of circuit campaigns. Anyway, I am not too sure it would be fair to subject professional handlers to their determined and stubborn characters. Many years ago at Pauline and Stanley Sharp's house in Patcham, we met a charming young man called Dana Hopkins. We were all so immersed in our doggy conversation we did not notice – and now cannot remember – if it was my three-year-old daughter Julia or Merry Princess that Dana had to rescue from Pauline's fish pond! Some years later I was delighted to meet Dana again in Illinois in 1981 showing his tri-colour Geraura's Wardlow, who took the Best of Winners on the day. Wardlow is a grandson of Castleray Sundance sent out to Dana by Norman Brown. Susan Cardenas used Wardlow to Ch Tudorhurst Gloriana's sister Ch Tudorhurst Candida and Dana and Susan have one puppy each. Wardlow was nine-years-old at the time. In spite of a busy law practice, Dana has always found time for his King Charles and many winning dogs in the States bear his Danho prefix.

Ch Geravras Wardlow. Best of winners at the Stokie Valley Kennel Club Show, 1981.

Ch Dreamridge
Dear Charles.

CHAPTER SEVEN

Toy Spaniels in Europe

WHEN Madame Francoise Guerin was offered a little King Charles Spaniel, Glenhurst Ludovicus, in the early Seventies, the breed was practically unknown in France. She was so entranced by the little dog that she decided to import several dogs to breed. Mrs Madeline Harper supplied a ruby dog and two black and tan bitches. The small ruby dog was Huntglen Red Paul, who became the first champion whole colour in France. Madame Guerin then imported Zepherine Tobias, from Mrs Joyce Birchall, a son of Ch Tudorhurst Simon, who soon became a champion, followed by Zepherine Bellette and Zepherine Hibiscus. From 1975 to 1987 Madame Guerin did all she could to foster and promote the King Charles Spaniel in France. From her imported stock she produced Ch Jude de Haute Lande, Ch Mike de Haute Lande, Champions Marmaduke, Ophelia and Omphale, all of de Haut Lande. Marmaduke bred to Zepherine Bellette produced an outstanding litter of three champions Pitchoun, Prince Georges and Petite Marche – all of de Haut Lande.

From Madame Guerin, Madame Biderman had Ch Mollie de Haut Lande and she imported Huntglen Black Prince from Mrs Harper, who became a French Champion. Madame Biderman showed her King Charles under the delightful prefix of Loving Dog. Madame Dereine also imported some black and tan King Charles from Mrs Harper but after a few years lost her interest in breeding.

Madame Perrein, another lover of the breed, imported her stock from Mrs Rita Evans of the Valevans and has recently been winning well with Valevan Jessica. Valevan Sir Pierre and Valevan Lady Fleur left England and Mrs Evans to join Madame Luc to become the foundation of the du Bois des Cauchee Kennel. More recently Madame Luc imported a bitch from Mrs Soper-Dyer of the Tregairn King Charles and a tri-colour dog from Mr and Mrs Byers.

In 1980 Madame Foutel bought her first King Charles from Madame

Guerin, who became Ch Penelope of Haute Lande. In 1986 a ruby dog from Mrs Diane Fry, Amantra Rosetermini, joined the Vallee du Soleil Kennels and became a French champion before leaving for America and the Dreamridge Kennels. In 1987 Mrs Pedley sent out to Madame Foutel a very attractive well-boned ruby dog, who won at the French Kennel Club Show at Toulouse. Ch Moordown Red Willow has proved to be a very worthy ambassador for the breed. Madame Foutel has recently imported from the States, USA Ch Dreamridge Dear Duncan, and from England she has bought Rossbonny the Gaffer, as well as several bitches, as yet unshown.

Madame Tournerie and Madame Jougneau are two of the more recent but enthusiastic breeders of King Charles. Madame Tournerie has turned to the Valevans for her foundation stock and Madame Jougneau is specialising in whole colour breeding. In 1981 Madame Sylvie Desserne bought from Madame Guerin the very beautiful Pitchoun de Haute Lande. He had a spectacular show career, becoming French champion, International champion, Belgium and Luxembourg Champion and both European and World champion. A particularly lovely dog, he won many admirers for the breed and, encouraged by his successes, Sylvie decided to breed King Charles Spaniels.

Three promising puppies by Cavella Royal Admiral out of Tudorhurst Black Magic. Owned and bred by Sylvie Desserne.

The obvious difficulty in establishing a breed in a foreign country is the numerically small gene pool available for breeding and it is important for the importer to know exactly what is available. It also helps if both importer and exporter have the same picture of what constitutes the ideal King Charles. Trust and friendship are essential ingredients for success. Lack of communication and understanding can only lead to disillusionment and failure. Sylvie's first two imports were the two Blenheims Tudorhurst Juliet and Tudorhurst Royal Tristram who both achieved their French and International Titles. But tragically Juliet died while undergoing a caesarean operation leaving a heart-broken Sylvie to hand-rear her first litter of King Charles. Tristram went on to produce three champions, Apple du Moulin de Genebret, Viking de Brunvale and Aurore du Close de la Vanne. Aurore is a very lovely tri-colour bred by Madame Jougneau and has been top winning bitch for the past two years.

From Holland Sylvie bought a Swedish-bred Blenheim bitch, Ch Jungfaltah Doreen Din. She was out of one of the last litters bred by the great Swedish breeder Mrs Erna Jungfeldt. Doreen is a lovely and typical King Charles full of charm and personality. She was bred to Sylvie's imported French Ch Amantra Escapade, a tri-colour bred by Mrs Lorraine Higgins, and produced Sylvie's first homebred champion, a very pretty little tri-colour Anais Nine de Vilfloriane. Then followed Int Ch Tudorhurst Royal Theodor, France's top winning King Charles for 1987 and 1988, Int Ch Tudorhurst Royal Charm, a Ch Moordown Morning Glory, daughter of my Tudorhurst Taffeta, Tudorhurst Black Magic, litter sister to Royal Theodor, both sired by Ch Zepherine Pierrot of Marbanks out of Ch Tudorhust Royal Theodora.

From starting with only two dogs in 1969 from Lady Forword's famous Eyeworth kennels, the Cavalier King Charles Spaniels in France have built up to an impressive entry of 140 at the 1988 Club Show.

Much of the praise can go to Madame Chevallereau, the President of the club. The club does all in its power to preserve and further the interests of the breed. The quality of the dogs I judged at the International Show in Rouen and the French Winners Show in Toulouse speaks well for the future. The honour of being the first French champion in 1975 went to Ch Ashpenda Double Diamond, owned and imported by Madame Chevallereau, and in 1978 his son Malcolme de la Dauderie became the first French Champion bred in France, owned by Madame Boulme.

In 1980 many breeders joined the dedicated band, among them M. Chiorino who built up a reputation for beautiful small compact dogs, sadly his early death was a tragedy for Cavaliers. The De Norlys prefix and some of the dogs will continue with M. Chiorino's partner. Cavaliers are considered one of the most important breeds in France at the moment. Madame Chevallereau's Des Mirkalines prefix is well to the fore and many notable and lovely dogs have borne this prefix. Madame Marchand has been breeding for five years and had made up five champions. In fact Bengy des Marliviers was Top Cavalier in 1988; he was my Best of Breed at the Winners Show in Toulouse where he went on to take the Toy Group. An exquisite small tri-colour, he has taken the championships in France, Luxembourg and Europe. Sired by one of the late M. Chiorino's dogs, Azzaro de Norlys, he is out of one of Mrs Diane Fry's kennel Amantra Heaven Sent. Ch Blenheim, daughter of his Dolly de Marliviers won the young class at the World Championship Show in Denmark.

At the French Winners Championship Show in Paris this year, Madame Marchand made their Dutch-bred Jorinde V H Lamslag a champion, bred by M. Boelaars. The judge was Miss Caroline Gatheral who went on to make M. Boelaar's Lodewijk V H Lamslag Best of Breed, a Dutch raid on the much-coveted French title. Madame Ducampe is another breeder who has benefited from M. Chiorino's de Norlys line. Madame Senechal du Domaine de la Source Enchantes and Belle de Nuit de la Source Enchantes achieved their French and World Championship.

Two English imports flying the flag for Britain are Madame Wendy L'Hote Sukev Trump Card, a very glamorous Blenheim champion, who won Best in Show at the 1988 Club Show and another Amantra owned by Madame Humphreys, called Amantra Flirtation. The French breeders say the breed has improved a lot since the early days when their first litters gave them long noses, bad fronts and very big dogs, but with experience and the help of some excellent imports they are pleased with the way the breed is progressing.

SCANDINAVIA

KING CHARLES SPANIELS

From the dawn of human life in Scandinavia, people have depended on animals. Cattle, sheep and hens have provided food, while horses and reindeer were used for transport. Hunting was a means of survival and so dogs of different breeds were also important. But from early on, there has been an interest in pets just for fun. Singing birds, exotic fishes, cats and toy dogs, all those pets that could be kept indoors during a long, cold and dark winter, have found their way into the Scandinavian household.

Toy dogs have always had a special place and this has been illustrated by writers and painters. Bolognese and Pugs are popular, but Toy Spaniels are without question on top. They have changed very little over the years,

*Courtisan painted
by David Kloeckner
Ehrenstraal, 1672.*

and not much distinguishes my King Charles Spaniels playing together on a sofa, from a picture painted in 1600.

At about the same time as King Charles II made the breed known throughout the world as *the dog that the King loves*, homes ranging from castles to cottages in Scandinavia included Toy Spaniels. The most well known are those that belonged to the Queen Dowager Hedvig Eleonora. In the Queen Dowager's huge collection of pets, the King Charles Spaniel seems to have taken a central place. Portrait paintings signed by David Kloecker Ehrenstraal show small spaniels with long coats, big round heads and dark eyes. One of them, named Courtisan, a beautiful red and white, was painted seven times, according to a cash-book. The Queen Hedvig Eleonora gave her spaniels French and Spanish names, like Don-Don, Plaisir and Gredlinetta, but her first dogs were imported from England.

In 1775 Hes Exellency Otto Fleming commissioned a painting of his black and tan King Charles. The dog is portrayed playing with a bumble bee, but it shows an unmistakable type. It is a small compact dog with a rich, straight coat. The head is big and the eyes wide and dark. The painting is full of grace and elegance. Posquin is the name of the King

Charles and the artist's name is Karl-Gustav-Pilo. It was some one hundred years later that breeders and owners combined to form the Swedish Kennel Club. This was launched with a dog show in 1886 in Stockholm. It is described as a well organised and successful event with 445 entries as well as some litters of puppies.

August Strindberg is famous for his literary works; he is not so well known for his dislike of dogs. In spite of this, or perhaps because of it, one of his wives, Siri Wrangel, left her King Charles Spaniel with him when she moved out. He described the dog, Mutte, as a monster!

One of the very few books written about the breed came from Norway. It is by Odd Hauers and is called *My Friend The King Charles Spaniel*. It was published in Oslo in 1953. But King Charles Spaniels were well established a long time before that in Norway. The first King Charles Spaniel shown in Norway was a dog called King. He was entered in the Norwegian Kennel Club show in Oslo in 1907. King was the Best Toy Dog in the group. He was bred in Leipzig and owned by Mrs Margit Hoeg.

The King Charles Spaniels also had their admirers in Sweden from early 1900. The Assarstorp Kennel started in about 1902, and the dogs from this kennel were well known in the show rings during the Twenties and Thirties. It is not uncommon to see generations of dogs with this breeding made into champions. The ruby Champion Isabell of Assarstorp, bred from Ch Muck of Assarstorp and Ch Millie II of Assarstorp, is one example. Dogs were imported mostly from the Ashtonmore and Breamore Kennels in England, but they also brought in dogs from Norway, from the Egra and Rosedell Kennels. The Toyhomes became well known and included Ch Toyhomes Susanna, a Blenheim, and Ch Toyhomes Sweet Dorothy, a black and tan. The Toyhome Kennel is still breeding toy dogs and has been a leader in the breed for nearly sixty years.

From the beginning of 1940 there were very few King Charles Spaniels in Scandinavia. The principal reason was distemper. It took some years for the breed to recover from the devastation of this terrible disease, but by the late Sixties and early Seventies the King Charles Spaniel witnessed a new renaissance in Scandinavia. Ch Zepherine Arraghslea Ilya was exported to Finland by Mrs Joyce Birchall. From Finland Ilya moved to Sweden to Mrs Maj-Lis Larsson and was mated to Ch Tangee of Huntglen and in this union he sired Ch King Carlos, a tri-coloured dog. It is not an understatement to say that King Carlos formed the cornerstone of the breed in Scandinavia. King Carlos sired Ch Achilles Attractive and Ch Amorina Surprise. In a repeat mating she produced two remarkable sisters. Bluebell and Belinda, both tri-coloured. Neither were shown much and never gained their titles, but they both won a best in show with several years between. At that time the King Charles were sharing a breed club with the Cavalier King Charles Spaniels. In 1982 a separate club was set up for breeders and owners of King Charles Spaniels in Scandinavia. It was called the King Charles Alliance and it organises a show every year and sends out a newsletter. The average number of entries is twenty to thirty, but on the fifth anniversary in 1987 there was a record number of fifty-three entries.

Kurt E. Ogevall

CAVALIER KING CHARLES SPANIELS

The early imports to Sweden laid the foundations of the success story of the Swedish Cavalier King Charles Spaniel. One of the most influential being Int Ch and Nordic Ch Kingmaker of Ttiweh, who sired Ch Edward of Knightlow before he left these shores to found a dynasty in Scandinavia: nine of his children became champions. Some of those early ambassadors were Ch Festival of Sunninghill, Ch Hillbarn Ian, Ch Welland Valley Solomon, Ch McGoogans Royal George of Hillhurst, Ch Cherry Court Tambourine, Ch Cherry Court Moonraker, Ch Lively Lady of Eyeworth, Ch Peter of Blagreaves, Ch Strawberry Fair of Carapace and Ch Alansmere Margery Doll, to name just a few.

In 1972 Margot Wrehammer and her husband Curt fell under the Cavalier spell, after many years of German Shepherds. Their first Cavalier, was Hojdens Honettan, a Blenheim, described by them as a wonderful bitch and the grandmother of their lines. From Diana Maclaine they imported the winning young dog who was to become one of Sweden's most successful sires Int and Scan Ch Trademark of Lochbuie. From the Hojdens kennels Curt and Margareta Brickman had their first Cavalier and have since built up a strong kennel of their own under the Gnistans prefix. Lillemor Andersson started in Cavaliers in 1974 and deciding to concentrate on whole colours she purchased from Diana Maclaine the outstanding ruby, now in his twelfth year, Jehufe Fire out of two black and tans, Louchbuie Macheath and Aldersbrook Cillas.

For the past twenty-one years the Sperringgardens Kennels have been famous for Cavaliers. They now boast a kennel of fifty-two Swedish Champions and fifteen International Champions, which has made them top breeders since 1985. Crisdig Pumpkin, bred and exported in 1975 by Mrs Susan Burgess, sired by Ch Crisdig Harlequin (another Ch Crisdig Celebration son) and out of a Celebration granddaughter Ch Crisdig Buttons. Crisdig Pumpkin stamped his soundness and quality on his progeny making him one of the most influential stud dogs in Scandinavia.

Apricot Fortuna by Int Ch Homerbrent Limelight has also enjoyed considerable success at stud, siring Int Ch Sperringgarden Cylvester and Int Ch Sperringgarden Cegovia. Int Ch Pennygown Coft Centre bred by Sheena Maclaine in England has had an outstanding show career, and I was delighted to watch him win the Toy Group after I had judged him Best of Breed in Upsala. Lochbuie Mary Maker, an English import, is the only tricolour to have achieved her international status.

Both Kristina Hellsen and Christina Wendel have founded their kennels on Sperringgarden. Cabina and Cimone, two Blenheim half-sisters belonging to Kristina Hellsen have achieved their titles and Cylvana, belonging to Christina Wendel, after achieving her title, produced a litter of six puppies to Coft Centre. Over the years Sissi Ledin has imported Cavaliers from Holland and England with considerable success but her present champion is Sperringgarden Comforter.

The Hazel White kennel of Gertrude Andersson founded in 1980 achieved success with Reserve Best in Show at the Swedish Kennel Club Championship Show with Hazel White Snowy Swede, a dog line bred to Crisdig Celebration through Sperringgarden stock. Anniette Almgren of Kennel Monsieur's has specialised in tricolours since 1978, although owning a few Blenheims as well. She based her bloodlines on Sissi Ledine's Leading Kennel, and the influential Lamslag kennel from Holland as well as the Sperringgarden kennel. The Rodeo Kennel of Laila (Lansberg) Larsson has imported several dogs from leading English kennels, her most recent import from the Kindrum kennels of Mrs Pamela Thornhill Ch Kindrum Gillespie won the 1989 Club Show judged by Mrs Molly Coaker.

Amantra, Cinola, Salador, Cottismeer and a host of other kennels have all played their part in achieving the excellent quality of the Swedish Cavalier. A special mention must be made of Homerbrent Handy Man, a little Cavalier who is hitting the highspots in the obedience world and has recently been filmed performing his feats; this delightful little dog so full of personality has made many friends for the breed.

Swedish Ch Maibee Alberto.

Int Ch Pennygown Coft Centre.

CHAPTER EIGHT

Breeding

GREAT Britain has always had the reputation for breeding some of the best dogs in the world. Possibly one of the reasons is that best British breeders have a natural flair or eye for spotting the potential great dog, and making the ultimate use of its assets. Although breeders are now learning and taking advantage of the terrific scientific advances in genetics and rearing, dog breeders in the UK have been far slower to listen to the scientists, than in other forms of animal husbandry. There is still a tendency to rely on inborn instincts. If they could couple this with the knowledge now available, the result would be better and sounder dogs, both physically and mentally. Dog breeding is a marvellous hobby, full of interest and excitement. The companionship of the dogs and the friends you make with the same interests make it all worthwhile. It certainly will not be for financial gain! I suspect more dog breeders are in the red for their love of dogs than I would care to mention.

My advice to anyone wanting to start breeding and showing Cavaliers or King Charles Spaniels, would be to read and learn all about both breeds, attend a few dog shows, watch and listen. Start slowly. If you merely want to exhibit, try to obtain a young dog with show potential. You are more likely to obtain a young dog with the makings of a winner, than a young bitch. It is not very often a breeder sells a truly outstanding bitch, as the breeder will naturally wish to retain the best bitches for breeding. Discuss with breeders the possibility of obtaining a good, sound, well-boned bitch puppy, remembering that the strength of any kennel lies in its bitches. Your bitch puppy must have a perfect temperament as well as being sound, well-boned and typical. If a bitch is bad-tempered or nervous, the puppies will imitate her and learn her bad behaviour.

Breeding a litter is a serious undertaking, and no one should embark on such a venture without first considering everything it entails. Breeding a litter is a long-term responsibility with far-reaching results: the future generations will carry the successes and failures. Each puppy receives from its grandparents 25 per cent of its inheritance and this will be halved in each successive generation until inheritance from great, great, great grandparents is $3\frac{1}{8}$%. Nature has taken care that each pup in a litter is an

*Tudorhurst Tiarella
at five weeks.*

David Barker

individual and receives a different combination of genes. Unless they are identical twins, which is fairly rare, the progeny of litter sisters can be quite different even if sired by the same dog.

Many breeders have used the method of in-breeding – the breeding together of close relatives, sire to daughter, dam to son, or brother and sister. The idea of in-breeding is to duplicate and fix the best points, and so breed a super-race. This would be ideal if both parents were perfect in temperament, conformation and constitution and, of course, carrying the genes for this perfection. Unfortunately, the unfavourable genes are just as likely to be duplicated, and also a recessive fault can appear. This can actually help the breeder to be aware of the bad faults their stock carries as well as the good. Prolonged in-breeding can eventually reach such a dangerous degree that all stock that is produced is degenerate. The danger signs are poor temperament, poor constitution and lack of fertility. In-breeding should only be undertaken by experts with many years' experience of their breed and by those with the strength of mind to destroy the faulty puppies that occur. In Cavaliers and King Charles there are now a sufficient number of good dogs for such a drastic programme to be unnecessary.

Tudorhurst Tamora and her sister Tudorhurst Thaisa at six weeks with their parents Castleray Buccaneer (left) at twelve months and Tudorhurst Thomasina.

Thomas Fall

Ch Tudorhurst Tamora (left) at eight months.

Thomas Fall

Line-breeding, which is another selective form of breeding, is a modification of in-breeding. The results are slower but far less dangerous. The idea of line-breeding is to maintain a close link throughout the pedigree with one or more individuals of outstanding merit. Once again, only dogs of the highest standard should be used. Line-breeding, if sensibly followed, is the basic formula used by many of the best kennels in the country. But again, there is a danger that it can be carried to such a degree that it borders on in-breeding and brings forth all the disasters of an ill-chosen in-breeding plan.

Occasionally out-crossing is necessary to improve or introduce a feature lacking in a strain of closely bred animals. In King Charles Spaniels it is practically impossible to have a complete out-cross, as all the present-day King Charles come from the small gene pool available after the war. With the much wider gene pool available in Cavaliers there are many strains built up entirely separate from each other.

Another method available is random breeding. This is when a breeder mates his bitch to a good dog which he likes for its good points, but is in no particular way related to his animal. It is of course essential that the animals complement each other and that they do not carry the same fault. A simple rule: Never breed from the same fault twice. For anyone wanting

*Ch Tudorhurst
Tamora full grown.*

Thomas Fall

*King Charles litter
at five weeks.*

David Barker

Ch Tudorhurst Simon at eight weeks.   Ch Tudorhurst Rebecca and Rachel.

a detailed and well written book on genetics, *The Dog Breeder's Introduction to Genetics* by Dr Eleanor Frankling is easy to understand, and ideal for those like me, who find science a mystery and the language of science totally incomprehensible!

Using the relatively simple laws of dominant and recessive genes, it is possible to understand the mode of inheritance and some of the faults that beset Cavaliers and King Charles. It is also possible to see why a dog or bitch occasionally emerges which has a major impact on the breed. A dog or bitch of this kind owes its prepotency to the fact that it is genetically pure, Because of its high degree of genetic purity, its progeny will possess the dominant parent's good points, no matter what faults their dams may show or carry. the offspring of a stud dog of this type, may resemble the sire, but they will also be carrying the recessive genes contributed by their dam. Exactly the same holds true for the prepotent bitch, except the impact by a dog is usually far greater by virtue of the number of puppies he sires.

Although you can endeavour to breed from the best possible stock available, I find it is to my Veterinary Surgeon that I turn for advice. When my pups are ready for their first inoculation my vet gives all the pups a thorough examination. He checks heart, eyes and limb joints and in male pups he ascertains that both testicles are fully descended and checks for the presence of inguinal and umbilical hernias. Four weeks later, when the pups are ready for their second inoculation, they are thoroughly examined again. Using the vet's specialised knowledge combined with my own judgement and experience, I have a good chance of detecting early faults. I would view with suspicion muscles which are tight on the inside of the thigh, limbs which rotate out of the straight, uneven strides, dogs which are close behind, and any peculiar or unusual gait. Pups learn very quickly to compensate and so mask disabilities which could be disastrous in a breeding programme. It certainly pays off to spend a lot of time with young pups watching and playing, for their enjoyment and education, as well as your knowledge of their potential.

As soon as your King Charles pups are born and you are rubbing them dry with a towel you will find you can pick the truly outstanding head. The head is well domed and the face, even at this age, is full, fat and square with a well-padded muzzle. Nose placement is of the utmost importance. In a good head the nose is in line with the eyes. The eyeline when viewed from the front is perfectly straight. Once you have seen this head at birth you will not forget it. Quite often these pups also have fused feet. The poor head will appear down-faced. The well-sprung ribs and short, chunky

Barham puppies.

Thomas Fall, 1938

Ashtonmore youngsters at ten weeks.

Thomas Fall, 1938

little legs are all obvious at birth. At five days it is not unusual for King Charles pups to open their eyes, and the majority will probably have their eyes fully open when they are a week old.

King Charles pups develop very rapidly and by three weeks their characters begin to emerge. This often surprises Cavalier breeders who have both breeds. By eight weeks you will begin to get a picture of the dog and by experience you will be able to get a clear idea of its development. If any structural faults appear at this age, I doubt very much they will improve; certainly bone and construction will not change. Mouths should be checked to see there is plenty of width between the eye teeth. The mouth should be slightly undershot, with no deviation either way. On both Blenheims and Tri-colours the markings can appear to change: often a narrow blaze at birth can disappear as the black and red hair encroaches on the white. By twelve weeks markings are fairly obvious, although the odd beauty spot on the face and freckles on the body and legs may appear at a later date. It is interesting to note that while King Charles breeders feel that the facial freckles or beauty spots enhance and give character to the

Tudorhurst Benedict at twelve weeks. He is now in France.

David Barker

Ch Curtana Morgana at eight months.

Thomas Fall

King Charles, the Cavalier breeders expect clean distinct markings with no freckling on the face or legs.

With Black and Tans and Rubies a small fine blaze on the head or chest will often completely disappear by adulthood. The richness of the tan colouration in all four colours is usually visible at birth except with Blenheims, who usually deepen by five weeks and certainly by twelve weeks. The poor tan carried by some whole colours is quite difficult to eradicate from your breeding programme. The same holds true for the pigment of the nose and eye rims. Once again, I would expect these to have darkened by five weeks and certainly by twelve weeks. After twelve weeks the pups appear to grow at different stages: one minute they are up on the leg and the next their bodies seem to lengthen to Dachshund-like proportions. The face which once looked so full and promising, now looks pinched and small. Just when you are about to despair, your butterfly emerges from the chrysalis with some degree of its former promise. King Charles are slow to reach their final stages of maturity, many being as late as three years before they fulfil their potential.

Cavalier pups, like King Charles, can display an outstanding head at birth. The head needs to be square, flat on top with no tendency to doming. The width of the skull and the width of the muzzle should be the same and balanced. The muzzle should also be well cushioned and filled

Tudorhurst King Charles puppies.

Thomas Fall, 1975

up underneath the eyes; the face should never appear pointed. The fine-pointed muzzle will never cushion up. The underjaw should be well filled, with good height and width. The line of the eye will give a good indication of the size of the eye. After a few weeks the well-cushioned soft square face will fill even more, while the others will appear to fall away. Length of ribbing is also apparent: there should be good width across the hindquarters, with thick thighs. If the thigh is narrow, the pup will often have a long hock. The best pups appear chunky and heavily boned from birth. The fine type tend to become too refined, while the heavier pup will often fine down. Markings, as with the King Charles, are apparent at birth, but blazes, particularly in the Tri-colour, will appear to narrow and diminish. Unbalanced head markings in the broken colours can give an odd appearance to an otherwise nice-looking pup. As with the King Charles, the nose and eye pigment should be black by five weeks. Lack of good pigmentation is an inherited fault and is hard to eradicate.

By six weeks you should have a happy, extrovert pup; reject the dejected, nervous pup that shies away. Always be advised by the breeder as to the character of the pups, as the breeder sees them all the time. By now most things are apparent: width of chest, length of leg (length of hock gives a good indication of the length of leg), rear movement, and set of tail – but not tail carriage. As a general rule, pups tend to carry their tails high

Cavalier King Charles Ch Homerbrent Bewitched at four weeks.

*Ch Homerbrent
Bewitched, full
grown.*

*A litter of Cavalier
puppies at eleven
weeks, sired by
Charlottetown Inigo
Jones.*

Leslie Ward

Puppies sired by Ch Homerbrent Carnival out of Ronnoc Solitaire of Homerbrent.

Pargeter Thunger Jet with puppies.

Thomas Fall, 1954

for the first three or four months. But if they are narrow behind and have a long hock, it is almost certain they will have a gay tail and they are frequently cow-hocked as well. Mouths can be a headache in Cavaliers, as so often at six weeks the mouth can be level or slightly undershot. But by the time they change their teeth, the bite can correct itself miraculously. Equally, the perfect mouth at eight weeks can go wrong with the change of teeth. But if the muzzle appears correct from the outside, and the bottom jaw does not jut out showing the bottom lip, there is a chance that with the change of teeth the mouth will be perfect. Mouth development tends to vary with the different bloodlines.

Little Breach puppies.

Thomas Fall, 1964

Colour Breeding

THE richness of the four recognised colours of the King Charles and Cavalier, tri-colour, Blenheim, black and tan and ruby is one of the great beauties of these little spaniels and any deviation from the desired colours is unacceptable in both breeds. In all four colours, the pigment of the nose and eye-rims should be black. The inheritance of coat colour depends on the Mendellian theory of dominant and recessive genes. The exception to this rule is the rare occurrence of mutation. Once such a change occurs, the new mutant gene can perpetuate itself with the same tenacity as the original genes. If anyone wants to make a detailed study of the mode of inheritance of coat colour, I would suggest they read Clarence Little's *The Inheritance of Coat Colour in Dogs*.

It has long been accepted by breeders of both varieties that the best results are obtained by breeding together tri-colour and Blenheim and black and tan and ruby. If broken colours and whole colours are crossed, there will be some mis-marked puppies, but if bred correctly these mis-marked puppies can be very useful in a serious breeding programme. I have taken each colour separately to illustrate what might be expected by crossing the four colours.

Blenheim to Blenheim: All Blenheims.

Blenheim to tri-colour: Both colours will appear, the percentage depending on the parentage of the dogs: if the tri-colour is tri-colour bred there will probably be more tri-colours; but if Blenheim bred, Blenheims will predominate.

Blenheim to black and tan: If the black and tan is whole colour bred, mis-marked black and tans and mis-marked rubies will predominate. Occasionally, a perfectly marked black and tan or ruby will appear. If one of the black and tan's parents is of broken colour breeding, it is possible for all four colours to appear.

Blenheim to ruby: Mainly mis-marked rubies with the occasional Blenheim.

Tri-colour to tri-colour: Mainly all tri-colours but occasionally Blenheims appear, if the tri-colours are Blenheim bred. Repeated over a long period tan will diminish.

Tri-colour to black and tan: If the black and tan is whole colour bred, mainly mis-marked black and tans will predominate. If the tri-colour is Blenheim bred, occasionally a mis-marked ruby will result. Very occasionally, a perfectly marked black and tan. I have not found this a very satisfactory combination.

Tri-colour to ruby: If the ruby is a dominant whole colour, there will be mainly mis-marked black and tan and mis-marked rubies, with the occasional perfectly marked black and tan or ruby. Blenheims and tri-colours can also appear.

Ruby to ruby: All rubies, but some may have small amounts of white on the chest or a few white hairs on the head, particularly if repeated over a long period. Richness of colour may diminish.

Ruby to black and tan: Black and tans and rubies. Some may have a small white patch on the chest or a few white hairs on the head, once again depending on the amount of broken colour in the ancestry.

Black and tan to black and tan: Usually all black and tan, but if repeated over a long period the tan will diminish and pale and white markings will appear.

Blenheim to mis-marked black and tan: Some very richly marked tri-colours and Blenheims, and also some mis-marked.

Tri-colour to mis-marked black and tan: Usually rather unsatisfactory as mainly heavily marked tri-colours and mis-marked black and tans.

Tri-colour to mis-marked ruby: Again some very richly marked Blenheims and tri-colours, as well as some mis-marked whole colours.

Blenheim to mis-marked ruby: Mis-marked rubies and the occasional well marked Blenheim.

Whole colour to mis-marked whole colour: The occasional perfectly marked whole colour with a predominance of mis-marked, but decreasing with each succeeding generation. In some cases, the inheritance factor of mis-marked whole colours can be treated as broken colours, albeit heavily marked: a mis-marked ruby of Blenheim parentage bred to a black and tan could produce all four colours, particularly if the black and tan has broken colour in its ancestry. Therefore, it is essential to know the colour of the ancestors of the dogs to be bred.

Some years back in the mid-Sixties we received a phone call on a Sunday afternoon from Mrs Molly Marshall of the Kormar Cavaliers who had a visitor from the Norwich area with a liver-coloured King Charles, or so it appeared to be. The lady insisted it was a Prince Charles, and she claimed she had papers to prove it. With detailed directions on how to get to our house, Molly sent her on her way. With camera primed and tea laid on, we waited and waited. The lady and dog must have disappeared in a puff of smoke en route. Both Molly and I tried to track her down, but to no avail. I knew of chocolate-coloured and white and tan Cavaliers, obviously mutants, but a chocolate-coloured King Charles I had to see!

Colour breeding was always one of Molly's many interests. She bred some very typical small black Cavaliers, so like the Mignard painting. At one time we saw several of these extremely pretty small all-black Cavaliers at Kormar, as well as a black and white who was used extensively at stud to all four colours of Cavalier. When the Cavalier King Charles Spaniel Club decided blacks and black and whites were totally unacceptable, Molly naturally ceased to breed blacks and black and whites.

To my knowledge, blacks and black and whites have never emerged in King Charles Spaniel breeding. To my horror, I had what can only be described as a blue and tan turn up in a whole colour litter of very mixed parentage; I took it as a sign of a lethal gene and ceased breeding from that line. Miss Vincent of the Vihurst told me she had a similar occurrence in 1939; she had also decided it was a mutant. The bitch's breeder assured me she had never had such an occurrence, but another breeder with a close relative of my bitch had the same experience. There is no shame in having the odd peculiar phenomenon turn up in your breeding programme, but a lot of heartache would be saved if people were honest and gave warning of the possible consequence of certain matings.

THE STUD DOG

THE owner of a stud dog has two responsibilities: one to his breed and the other to his dog. As far as the breed is concerned, the stud owner should never accept a bitch that lacks quality and type, as without these attributes the chances of producing puppies that will enhance the breed are minimal. To protect his dog the owner should carefully vet the health, cleanliness and temperament of the prospective bitch, as any infection could render the dog sterile. As the owner of a stud dog, you have the right to refuse any bitch you wish.

In my early days in King Charles Spaniels, I campaigned Homehurst Merry Monarch. When he was barely a yearling he won Best Toy and finished Reserve Best in Show at an open show and he also had a challenge certificate to his credit. Naturally, we were very proud of him and excited about his prospects. At the open show, a young man introduced himself to me as a judge and professional handler; he complimented me on Monarch and asked me if he had been used at stud. I explained that both Monarch and I were extremely green in that field. The young man stressed that it was absolutely essential to start as soon as possible. He said he had just the right bitch which he would bring over that evening – he and his friend would take care of the mating. He also pointed out that it was customary not to charge a fee for unproved young dogs. Slightly perturbed by the young man's persistence, I asked for time to return home to feed my family, dogs and husband! Once at home I immediately phoned my friend and mentor Mrs Violet Jackson and said I was uneasy about the situation, although it was also quite possible that the young man was being kind and genuinely wanted to help. Within the space of half-an-hour I had received three phone calls from well established and respected members of the breed who had been alerted by Mrs Jackson. They were all aware of the young man and his bitch which was of the most dubious ancestry, with only the merest whisper of a King Charles. In those days it was possible to get Class II registration at the Kennel Club for unregistered dogs of any ancestry, provided two judges gave an undertaking that the dog resembled the required breed. This was a rather short-sighted and dangerous practice, which fortunately ceased some time ago. I explained to the young man that I had been advised of his bitch's bloodlines and I could not possibly countenance the creation of a mongrel litter. In those days the telephone was manually operated and our local operator often joined in the conversation. That night I fear he learnt a few words that were quite new to me. It was all extremely unpleasant and I decided then and there that my dogs would not be at public stud. The young man went abroad and died some years ago.

I need not have worried about not putting my dogs at public stud: Monarch had already decided he only had one love in his life, and that was Tudorhurst Rhapsody of Ainsleyfield (Tessa). When he was confronted by Araminta of Lavenderway, the owner was sure that Araminta's charms and experience would lure Monarch; but just in case she also brought a miniature bottle of rum. All to no avail — Monarch fled from chair to chair hotly pursued by Araminta. Eventually he sought sanctuary on the sofa table, and in desperation I drank the rum!

It is important to remember that the visiting bitch is on strange ground and will be apprehensive. She will need time to relax and settle. Introduce her to the dog, making sure she has a collar and lead so she can be restrained if she attempts to snap. If there is a great height difference

The Breed's leading Stud dog Ch Homeranne Caption.

between the dog and the bitch, you may have to help out with a piece of matting, towelling or the odd telephone directory. Once the dog and bitch are tied they must not be left unattended: it is not unknown for a bitch to suddenly turn on the dog. Some King Charles dogs appear to faint after they have tied. Do not be alarmed, as they recover after a few seconds. Some ties can be excessively long – one-and-a-half hours is not uncommon – so make sure you have a comfortable cushion to sit on and a good book. If you are worried the tie is too long and has gone on longer than ninety minutes, crushed ice applied to the affected parts usually does the trick.

With a maiden bitch it is advisable to give two matings, ideally with a day in between. As a general rule, the best time is between the tenth and fourteenth day after the bitch has come into season and started to show colour. It is usually when the colour of the discharge starts to change, becoming less brightly coloured. If the bitch is receptive to the dog, you have probably got the right day. If she is adamant that she will not be mated, do not attempt it; the chances are she will have problems anyway. Nature knows best.

It is well worth taking time to train a stud so that he is used to having his bitches held for him. It will save hours of time-wasting frustration. When the dog is about ten months old, introduce him to a mature experienced bitch, who is obviously ready. She will show this by stamping her feet and her tail will flag to one side. Once the dog has mounted her, hold the bitch and praise the dog. The confidence he gains from his first experience will stand him in good stead for future matings. Many dogs are slow to reach sexual maturity. Do not be worried, just keep trying. If for any reason your stud dog is consistently failing to sire puppies, ask your vet to do a sperm count. This is a very simple test, and if you are selling an adult as a stud dog, it is an invaluable exercise.

THE BROOD BITCH
THE old saying: 'A kennel is only as good as its bitches', holds a great deal of truth and every serious breeder wants a bitch that has quality and breeding, but above all, soundness and a sweet disposition. A lively, active animal is less likely to have breeding problems than a dim-witted, fat, sluggish bitch. The sire should be chosen for the quality of his progeny, rather than by his show record. Look to the dog for the qualities lacking in your bitch, and make sure he comes from stock that is free from hereditary faults and that he has been living in a healthy environment. Always have the courtesy to telephone the stud owner the day your bitch comes in season to arrange a suitable time.

Having achieved a successful mating, make sure your bitch is kept in a safe place, secure from roaming males. It is inadvisable to overfeed an expectant mother; in fact she will not need any change in her diet during the first six weeks. If she becomes very heavy she may appreciate having her food divided into small, more frequent meals because of the discomfort of being over-full. At six weeks in whelp we have all our bitches boosted with dead parvo virus vaccine, as a precaution. We have never found this has had any detrimental effect on the puppies and it does eliminate the risk of importing infection from shows or visiting friends which could harm the litter. At approximately the last five days of pregnancy, we start to give Canovel calcium tablets.

Our puppies are usually born in our bedroom. We have a large wooden whelping box which is lined with cardboard. We make a mattress with a board, place a heater pad on it, and cover it with Vetbed or equivalent bedding. This is firmly secured so the bitch cannot dig up the bed and bury the pups. The heater flex must be pushed through the cardboard and up between the cardboard walls and the whelping box to discourage the puppies from chewing it. After each litter we burn the bedding and cardboard, scrub the whelping box with Domestos and then we are ready to start again!

It is very important to keep the bitch well exercised right up to her whelping. She needs to be well muscled. Gentle exercise, plenty of fresh air and a sensible diet will prepare her for motherhood. It is a great help if you can find an experienced breeder to advise you with your first litter. The most common signs of a bitch going into labour are panting, bed-making and an increased restlessness. A waterbag usually heralds the arrival of the first puppy, which travels into this world coated in membrane with its afterbirth attached. Make sure that you have all the afterbirths at the end of whelping, as a retained afterbirth can cause metritis which may result in the death of your bitch. Quite often puppies are born tail-first, and you will have to assist the bitch by gently drawing the puppy away. A piece of soft towelling or flannel will help you to get a grip of the slippery pup. When the pups are born, rub them vigorously head-down with a towel until they squeak. We have two pairs of artery forceps, both well sterilised. One pair is used to clamp on the umbilical cord, making sure it is not too short, and the other pair is used to gently shred away the afterbirth and remaining cord. If the bitch shreds the umbilical too close and the puppy is in danger of rupturing, have some linen thread ready and tie off the cord and then dust with wound powder. But usually, the clamping of artery forceps will stop the bleeding.

If the bitch appears to be having difficulty giving birth, do not hesitate to call your vet. Any delay can cause the death of your bitch and her pups.

If your bitch has to have a caesarean, make sure she has recovered from the anaesthetic before you give her the puppies, as she may inadvertently lie on them. Soon after the birth of the pups, check them over carefully for any deformities. Cleft palates and hare-lips are fairly obvious but occasionally some of the internal organs are outside the body. In fact, I had this horror with my first litter, an only pup. In my ignorance, I tied up with linen thread and cut away what I thought was excessive afterbirth and cord, only to find I had cut off the internal organs. Luckily my vet was with me in a few minutes. The decision whether or not to rear a malformed puppy is one of the hardest to make, but I would always advise against. The breeds can certainly do without these sub-standard specimens, and you will be left to look after them for the remainder of their life. They will certainly be your responsibility and, ultimately, your heartbreak.

Hind dew claws can escape notice, but these should be removed within the first few days of birth by your vet. In the early stages make sure all the pups are kept warm, and when you take the bitch out for exercise, cover them with a light piece of blanket. Chilled pups will cry and whinge constantly and do not seem to thrive.

When you are sure the bitch has finished whelping and has expelled all the afterbirths, offer her a little warm milk and honey. Later on a small meal of stewed rabbit will go down very well. Keep the diet light and easily digested for the first few days. Make sure the pups feed from all the teats

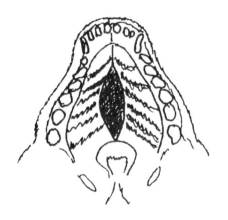

Cleft Palate.

or you will suddenly find yourself with a very uncomfortable dam with engorged teats. We have found a Milk of Magnesia tablet a day for the first week a great help; it is supposed to neutralise acidic milk.

Eclampsia must be watched for with nursing bitches. The tell-tale signs are panting and a curious twitching of the limbs. Any general discomfort or uneasiness should be treated as suspicious; the bitch will start to stagger and eventually go into fits. It is important to get her to the vet in the early stages, when she will be given calcium intravenously. If the condition is caught early, the recovery is instant, but the bitch must be watched at all times. Keep her quiet, and it may be necessary to ease the strain on her by removing the puppies altogether or by giving them supplementary feeds. Your vet will advise.

Typical Breeding Stock.

Thomas Fall

CHAPTER NINE

Feeding and Rearing of Puppies

THE feeding and rearing of puppies, as with all young animals and babies is a mixture of commonsense, patience and having an awareness of forthcoming problems and preventing them. The truly good stockman, with a natural affinity to animals, is a natural, but that does not mean you cannot be trained to be aware of the needs and difficulties of young animals. Vigilance is one of the golden rules.

At birth, all that tiny puppies require is warmth, peace and quiet, and a full tummy. Provided the bitch has a plentiful supply of milk, the early days should be troublefree and you will watch your puppies grow rapidly day by day. They should look fat, sleek and contented. If you have to hand-rear or supplementary-feed a large litter, I have found the following mixture to be the best (but there are plenty of proprietary brands available):

> One tablespoon boiling water
> One saltspoon honey
> One tablespoon Ideal milk
> Five drops Dinnefords gripe water

During the first few hours it is essential to see that all the pups are feeding well and regularly and that the larger pups are not pushing their smaller littermates from the milk bar. Sometimes pups born by Caesarean section are slower to feed initially than those from a troublefree whelping. The trauma of birth seems to slow them down. Some maiden bitches are very restless for the first few days and will require constant supervision, but given time, and with patience, they suddenly awaken to the joys of motherhood. Make sure the bitch is cleaning her pups; if not, you will have to be surrogate mother. Using a swab of cotton-wool, dampened in warm water, gently massage the pup's stomach. Repeat the whole procedure massaging under the tail. A little smear of Vaseline under the tail also helps to stop the faeces sticking. If you are hand-rearing orphan puppies, they will need to be fed at two-hourly intervals, using approximately two teaspoonfuls at each feed night and day. Small feeding bottles for puppies are available and, as with babies, all feeding utensils need to be soaked in sterilising fluid when not in use. Keep a close check on puppies' nails from about three weeks onwards. They can become exceedingly sharp and scratch the mother when they feed, as well as damaging each other's eyes when they are playing.

Happy contented puppies grow and flourish. At about three weeks we start to give our puppies a little scraped raw beef about the size of a marble, gradually increasing the amount until at four weeks they are having scraped or finely minced beef twice daily. This can be obtained by scraping a piece of lean beef steak with the edge of the spoon, and can be fed as early as seventeen days. Very lean, finely-minced beef can soon be substituted for the scraped beef. At four to four-and-a-half weeks, we introduce them to the milk mixture, thickened with a little first-stage baby cereal. We find it easiest to offer this from a teaspoon and once they have got the idea of lapping we put down a small bowl. This usually heralds a free-for-all and everyone falls in the mixture. It now seems a good time to start grooming them!

Try to keep the diet simple, as any undue drastic changes will upset the puppies' digestion. By five or six weeks, try a little Pedigree Puppy Chum, chopped chicken or scrambled eggs as an alternative to the mince. A Farley's baby rusk is always a great favourite with puppies. By the time they are six to seven weeks they should be having four or five small meals a day. Fresh water should be available from six weeks onwards. Choose your water bowl with care: it should be heavy so it is hard to knock over but small enough so as not to provide a paddling pool or a watery grave.

King Charles and Cavaliers are very easy to house-train. They are fastidiously clean by nature and dislike being dirty. If they are regularly popped outside after meals they quickly learn what is desired of them. But do not allow the pups to become wet and chilled. Worming is essential for all puppies. Antepar Liquid is available from any good chemist. The dosage is 5 ml for 10lbs of bodyweight, so you can adjust it accordingly. We worm our puppies at five weeks and seven weeks and again at eleven weeks. This fits in quite well with their inoculations at nine weeks and twelve weeks. If you notice any sign of diarrhoea or vomiting in young puppies or any signs of distress, ask your vet to call as soon as possible, otherwise he may be too late to be of any help. It must be very frustrating for veterinary surgeons to be presented with patients who have been subjected to treatments from unqualified people, and then be expected to work a miracle.

CHAPTER TEN

Adult Feeding

THE choice of feeding is very much one of personal choice and convenience. I have always fed fresh, raw meat and fresh tripe as well as a variety of cooked meats and as I have been pleased with the results, I can see no reason to change. There are a few excellent all-in-one diets on the market and having seen the lovely condition of some of the dogs fed on them I would never dare to criticise anyone else's method of feeding. A great deal depends on the availability of fresh meat in the area. If you can find a good butcher or slaughterhouse with a reliable and consistent source of meat, treasure it!

Our dogs also relish certain tinned meats but we prefer to use the best, such as Pedigree Chum. Most of the dogs can find a favourite among the many varieties. Denes Healthmeal is also excellent and so is the occasional tin of corned beef. For the first six months of a puppy's life and while a bitch is nursing a litter, we feed the best quality beef mince we can obtain. All our adult dogs have red meat at least twice a week, otherwise they have fresh tripe – cooked or raw – or beef, lamb or Pedigree Chum. A great favourite is lambs' or beef hearts with liver, cooked in a large casserole, sometimes with carrots, turnips or swedes and served with rice. Other tried and trusted options are chicken, turkey, or rabbit, boiled or casseroled. But obviously the bones must be removed. Sweetbreads make another welcome change, and sheep's heads, casseroled until the meat falls off the bone, gives a nourishing meal.

I met my Waterloo when our butcher suggested I tried a bullock's head. It was certainly a mammoth. It took all my strength to carry it from the car and the kitchen table practically buckled under the weight. There was no way it was going in the oven. I decided to cut off the nose portion. A freezer saw was useless, a fret-saw fell to pieces. Eventually, I had to sit on the head on the kitchen floor and use an evil-looking saw I found in the wood shed. It took ages. I forced the main portion of the head into the oven covered in foil, and I boiled the nose portion on top of the stove. It took hours to cool before I could take the meat off. The jaw bone was massive. The remaining skull could hardly go out in the dustbin so we had to bury it in the garden. So I do not recommend bullock's head unless you are Hercules!

If you can get rabbits, they are much appreciated, particularly by bitches just after whelping. In the autumn after the harvest rabbit shoots, we can often get a couple of dozen. We find if we put the head in a paper bag, they look a lot less like Peter Rabbit and we can get on with skinning and portioning them up for the freezer. Scrambled eggs, custard, rice puddings, sago, tapioca and macaroni cheese all make a pleasant change. Brands Essence of beef or chicken is very nourishing and easily assimilated; it will tempt an invalid or the most finicky feeder until the usual diet is acceptable. Dogs like variety as much as we do.

We feed biscuit separately. Always use the best quality biscuit available. Taste it yourself for freshness. Brown bread, cut into strips dipped in beaten egg, tossed in grated cheese and baked in the oven until crisp, is as good as any dog biscuit. Homemade dog biscuits are excellent and we find all our dogs like them. The following recipe was given to us by Miss Turner of the Jarrah King Charles Spaniels.

     1 lb wholemeal or stoneground flour or
     ½ lb wholemeal and ½ lb muesli
     6 ozs beef dripping
     2 tbs extract of malt, or West Indian treacle or grated cheese
Mix to a stiff dough with milk, buttermilk or sourmilk (¼ pint approx.). Roll out fairly thinly. Cut into the desired shapes and bake at approx. 300-350 until dried out and crisp.

We feed twice a day, at 7 am and 5 pm. It is more important to have a regular routine, rather than worry about the actual time. Fresh clean water should be available at all times. It is also advisable to give a good vitamin supplement. There are plenty to choose from.

CHAPTER ELEVEN

Grooming

BOTH King Charles Spaniels and Cavaliers are comparatively simple to groom. Regular brushing with a pure bristle Mason Pearson-type brush and careful combing through the fringes are all that is required, on a daily basis. Check that the eyes are clean and if necessary wipe with cotton wool, wrung out in Optrex. Make sure no food or dirt adheres to the pockets at the corners of the mouth, causing soreness and unpleasant odours. Check that the insides of the ears are clean, and then dust with Sherley's Canker Powder. If they are dirty or inflamed, obtain some drops from your veterinary surgeon. If you have a cat, grab it and do its ears as well. It will probably be the cat that is the carrier of the ear mites. Grass seeds can be a nuisance during the summer months. They become lodged inside the ears and between the pads causing pain and irritation which may need veterinary attention.

Regular bathing with Vetzyme Insecticidal Shampoo will keep the coat free of parasites and sweet-smelling. King Charles Spaniels and Cavaliers adapt very quickly to the use of the hair dryer. It is essential to make sure they are well dried before going out or they may become chilled. Nails need checking regularly. If necessary cut them, just taking the tips and avoiding the quick.

Constant scratching is not only irritating to the dog, but becomes a nuisance to the owner. Check for the obvious fleas and lice, and if in doubt give a bath using Tetmasol Soap or Alugan Wash. If the dog appears to have dandruff, do not just dismiss it as dry skin; it is quite possibly a tiny mite which causes skin scaling and you will need to use a veterinary-recommended shampoo. Country dogs often pick up the odd tick. The best way to get rid of them is to soak the tick in ether or surgical spirit. In an emergency, I have used my perfume neat (St Laurent Opium will make 'em gasp) or even a lighted cigarette – anything to make them release their hold long enough for you to pick them off intact with tweezers. If you do not remove the head part, it can cause infection.

If grooming and wellbeing go hand in hand, I cannot stress too strongly that all dogs should have plenty of exercise and space to develop their

Nails should be cut regularly so that only the tips need to be clipped. Exercise on hard surfaces, such as road-walking, will help to keep the nails in trim.

David Barker

personalities. King Charles Spaniels and Cavaliers need human companionship, their lives revolve around their owners. To starve them of attention would indeed be cruel.

The inside of a toe nail. It should be clipped at the top, avoiding the quick.

Do not forget to brush and comb the featherings on the legs, paying particular attention to the top and inside of the front legs and the upper part of the inside hindquarters.

David Barker

David Barker

Regular grooming with downward strokes will tone the body as well as keeping the hair free of tangles.

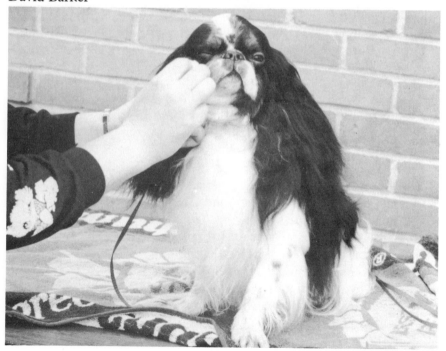

Wipe the face, paying particular attention to the eyes, and the stop when dealing with a King Charles. Use a cotton wool pad soaked in boiled water or Optrex and then wring out until it is moist.

CHAPTER TWELVE

Training, Exhibiting and Judging

BOTH King Charles Spaniels and Cavaliers are easy to train: they are responsive to their owners and very willing to please. Every dog, no matter what breed, should be acquainted with basic obedience. Just as children are educated in their formative years to prepare them for adulthood, so all puppies should be educated in the niceties of canine behaviour to prepare them for their adulthood. Both dog and owner should have pleasure in each other's company, and the dog should not be locked away in a kennel or room, bored and lonely. A well-behaved dog is also a happy animal, secure in its knowledge that it can cope with most situations.

For some strange reason, there seems to be a school of thought that dogs that attend obedience classes cannot be shown, as the discipline of obedience conflicts with show training. Perhaps some owners do not credit their dogs with enough intelligence. We have attended both obedience and show training classes and I would welcome the time to be able to attend more often. Mrs Mandy Wickens did competitive obedience with her King Charles and he acquitted himself equally well in the show and obedience rings. There are many Cavaliers that have also enjoyed both fields. Enjoyment should surely be the main reason for owning a dog.

Most young puppies learn at an early age to come when called, and particularly if they are rewarded with praise. The secret of training is to prevent bad habits developing; prevention is much better than cure. Teach the meaning of the word 'no' or 'leave': this will save destruction of chairs, slippers, shoes, tea towels and Grandma's best hat. Both King Charles and Cavaliers are sensitive to their owners' demands, and tone of voice is usually reprimand enough.

The critical stage in a puppy's development is between seven and fourteen weeks, when all puppies should be socialised, becoming accustomed to different noises, strangers, children and other animals. Do not allow visitors to force themselves on young dogs; allow the puppies to set the pace and make the initial overtures. Ignore shyness and never ever punish a puppy that shows fear. Ask visiting friends or children to sit on the floor to play with the puppy; accidents can so easily happen with a lively puppy leaping out of someone's arms. Do not scoop the puppy up in your arms every time anyone calls, as very soon your over-protective behaviour will transfer to the young dog and you will have a neurotic over-protective, snappy dog. As with children, use commonsense and foresee the situation as it develops and take steps to prevent trouble occurring.

If you do not have many visitors, join a training class; your local canine society will advise you of one that will suit your needs. There your puppy will learn to socialise with other breeds of dogs. Training classes are educative and fun, but make sure your puppy is fully inoculated. In a very short time the commands of down, stay and heel will be second nature to your puppy. The command of down and stay may even save your dog's life. When my aunt was staying with us some years ago, she took her King Charles, Leonora, litter sister to Simon, and a rather obstreperous young King Charles, for a walk round the fields. The rather badly behaved young King Charles decided to chase our geese, one of whom was excessively bad-tempered and would attack anything if she felt so inclined. Because my aunt had taken Leonora to obedience classes she was able to drop her in the down position, tell her to stay, and run across the fields to rescue the badly behaved youngster, who but for my aunt's speedy rescue would probably have met an untimely end.

When you start to lead-train your dog, teach him to walk without pulling right from the start. If you have allowed your dog to get away with this annoying habit, teach the dog to heel, and turn suddenly and frequently, so he does not have the chance to dash off. Having learnt basic obedience, your puppy is now ready to embark on a show career if you so wish. A show dog is not required to do a great deal but show off his charms so that the judge can see he is correctly constructed and is sound of limb, and fits the appropriate breed standard. To ascertain movement, the judge will ask that the dog be moved so that he can see hind movement, front movement and side movement; these usually take the forms of moving in a circle, triangle or just up and down. If the dog is taught to move in unison with the handler at a steady pace, he will display his movement and deportment to better advantage than the dog who dashes off spinning and weaving round the ring. The judge will also wish to give your dog a detailed appraisal on the table, so it will also help if you can train your dog to stand and stay on the table, while the judge checks his mouth, eye colour and general construction. Having struggled with King Charles that flatten like pancakes on the table, I really only have myself to blame for not taking the time to train them properly.

The Cavalier standing on a table, ready for the judge's inspection.

David Barker

The Cavalier free-standing.

David Barker

If a dog is reluctant to show, it may need some help from the handler in order to show to advantage.

David Barker

Assessing front movement.

David Barker

Assessing side movement.

David Barker

In order to attend your first show you must submit your entry on the appropriate form and the puppy must be registered under your name at the Kennel Club. Before the show, bathe your dog in good quality shampoo, like Vetzyme, and brush the coat flat while it dries. Always pay the judge the compliment of presenting your dog in the very peak of condition and in the best coat possible. The night before the show, pack your show bag with a brush, comb for grooming, cotton wool for cleaning the face, kitchen roll to clean up accidents, a towel to dry your dog, a show lead and a water bowl. It is not necessary to take water; most show grounds now have water laid on. A few dog biscuits are useful – as well as a dog blanket or cushion to make the dog comfortable. I always carry a bottle, opener and screwdriver, as inevitably someone always needs one, a packet of headache pills, a small bottle of Kaolin mixture for emergencies and Waspeeze for the wasp stings. In the height of summer, frozen towels or freezer bags can be a life-saver on excessively hot days. Eye ointment is another necessity, as well as disinfectant to wipe out your show bench. A ring card clip and a safety pin come in useful for other emergencies. The day you leave out one item to lighten the load is always the day you will wish you had brought it.

Some dogs are naturally good showers – in fact they have the ability to project their personalities and are born showmen. Ch Curtana Morgana was just such a dog. The moment she entered the ring, she blossomed. Other dogs, like people, have their on and off days. Ch Tudorhurst Royal Rebellion was one of these. As a young dog, he enjoyed showing; but as he grew older he became increasingly bored with the whole idea, and a couple of experiences of rough handling by heavy-handed judges did little to increase his enthusiasm. On one occasion a judge of some renown approached Rebellion from the rear, picked him up without any warning and promptly dropped him. Although the judge apologised afterwards, explaining he did not believe any dog with so much coat could have a well-developed muscled body underneath, the damage was done. After that, Rebellion never took his eyes off the judge, and he made sure he always faced the judge squarely: he was never going to be picked up so unceremoniously again! On another occasion, in the group judging, a lady judge got her gold charm bracelet entangled in his ears; if he had not been so good about letting us untangle the muddle I would probably have been able to come home with a very nice bracelet.

There is a lot more to dog showing than simply winning a prize. There is the anticipation and excitement, and there is great pleasure in meeting so many people interested in dogs and in your breed in particular. There are times when you will widely disagree with the judge. Try to accept defeat gracefully; the remedy is to never show under that judge again. If you have been unfairly treated, you will find there are other qualified spectators who will be just as quick to resent the injustice, and at the end of the day it will not be the loser who looks ridiculous. Even more poisonous than the bad-tempered loser is the boastful winner. Remarks like: 'We can't help winning, we have the best dogs,' are guaranteed to rub everybody up the wrong way. It is only one judge's opinion on that day; there is always another day and another judge.

Always make sure you have your ring number safely pinned on and do not keep the other exhibitors waiting by being late. Stand quietly with your exhibit and show your dog. There is no need to keep thrusting the dog under the judge's nose; in fact any display of bad manners is totally unacceptable. When the great Leo Wilson was judging King Charles, he became totally exasperated with a lady who kept picking her dog up and waving it about under the judge's nose. 'Madam, put your dog down, it can't walk on its head,' he advised.

With the inclement British weather, it is best to be prepared for all eventualities. Stiletto heels should be taboo at all times: not only could you seriously injure a dog with them, you will spike hall floors and sink into

The King Charles standing on a table, ready for the judge's inspection.

David Barker

Standing on a loose lead.

David Barker

Assessing side movement.

Assessing front movement.

Assessing back movement.

the grass. Sensible, comfortable shoes are a necessity. At one time, hats were worn by both exhibitors and judges. Tamora, who particularly enjoyed country life, once espied what she thought was a pheasant sitting on one well-known lady judge's head. When she was on the table with the judge bending over her, she deftly seized the hat and there ensued a very undignified tug-of-war between judge, dog and very embarrassed handler. The hat was retrieved, looking very battle-scarred, and plonked back on the judge's head.

After some years of exhibiting and breeding you will probably feel you would like to try your hand at judging. Most breed clubs advocate that an aspiring judge should have at least five years experience of successful breeding and showing before attempting to adjudicate. My advice would be to gain all the knowledge and experience you can, and I found one of the best ways was to steward for well-established breed judges and all-rounders. Most all-rounders are very generous with their help and advice. Not only will you learn ring procedure and the marking of judging books, you will gain valuable knowledge that will stand you in good stead for the future. Judging is a great responsibility that should not be undertaken lightly. The Kennel Club issue you with a breed standard and little else: the rest is up to you. Aspiring Cavalier judges are extremely

A King Charles can be taught obedience too!

Dalton

lucky, as their breed clubs run regular seminars to educate and instruct. With the burgeoning of interest in the King Charles, let us hope that their clubs will run more seminars. The interchange of ideas and experiences between breeders can only help to further the knowledge we all strive to gain.

On your first judging appointment, arrive early to give yourself time to settle. If you have time, read your breed standard again before you go in the ring. Once in the ring, take your time: handle each dog with care and give each dog sufficient time to settle and show to its best advantage. Above all, be fair and do not use your judging appointment to settle old scores. Evaluate each dog as you see it according to your interpretation of the standard.

CHAPTER THIRTEEN

General Ailments

IN order to keep your dogs in good health, it is most important that you have a good veterinary surgeon who will help and discuss your problems. Make sure that all your dogs are regularly vaccinated and wormed; your vet will advise you on the most up-to-date methods. The advice and information I can offer is not meant to be an alternative to veterinary treatment but should be seen as first-aid that may help in an emergency.

ABSCESS
This is a painful swelling which can be relieved by hot fomentation of salt water (one dessertspoon of salt to ½ pint of hot water). Bathe frequently with a cotton wool pad, which will encourage suppuration. Once the wound has opened it may be syringed out with equal parts hydrogen peroxide and water. If the abscess fails to open and drain, your vet will have to lance the swelling. During the summer, barley grass seeds can often cause abscesses.

ANAL GLAND
The anal glands sometimes become blocked and infected. It is a good idea to always check the anal glands whenever you bathe the dog and if necessary empty them. Get someone qualified to show you this very simple procedure. Some dogs are more prone to this problem than others. Make sure there is enough roughage in the diet to make the anal glands empty regularly and naturally. If the anal glands have become inflamed, it is essential to take the dog to the vet for swift treatment.

BAD BREATH
This is nearly always caused by tartar deposits accumulating on the dog's teeth. If you are unable to remove the tartar yourself with a tooth scraper you will have to make regular visits to the vet for scaling. It is naturally much better to clean the teeth yourself as your vet will have to give the dog an anaesthetic. Hard crunchy biscuits will help to keep the teeth clean. Swabbing the teeth and gums with a weak solution of hydrogen peroxide was a tip given me by Mrs Vincent of the Vihursts. At eleven years of age Ch Pierre Again had every sparkling little tooth in his head.

Burns

Apply cold water to ease the pain immediately. Never apply any ointment before your vet has seen the wound.

Colds

Occasionally during the winter months King Charles appear to have a little splashing from the nose, and the eyes appear to be runny. If the dog is kept dry and warm and the eyes are wiped with a little Optrex, all will be cleared up in a day or so. If not, seek veterinary advice. Feed garlic daily as a preventative.

Constipation

Liquid paraffin, approx one teaspoon, is the safest cure.

Coughs

If your dog develops a sudden cough, seek veterinary advice. In the first instance it may be kennel cough which will clear with veterinary treatment. Benylin, a human cough mixture, can help alleviate the condition. But cases of kennel cough must be isolated, as the cough is highly contagious and though not dangerous to adult dogs it can prove fatal to puppies and very old dogs. A cough may be a sign of heart condition and this will also need veterinary help.

Cysts (Interdigital)

Cysts are soft swellings between the toes which cause dogs irritation so that they are constantly licking. Sometimes the skin breaks and there is a discharge of watery blood. Bathe with salt and water or liquid garlic. A course of greenleaf tablets from Denes can also be helpful. Check for grass seeds. If the condition doesn't clear up, seek veterinary advice.

Dandruff

Make sure your dog is having enough fat or oil in the diet. If not, give one teaspoon of sunflower oil daily. Scurf is also caused by a tiny parasite which causes the skin to flake. A good medicated wash such as Alugan or Hexayl, can be obtained from your vet, or from the chemist.

Diarrhoea

If this is caused by a dietary allergy or sudden change of food, rest the stomach for twelve hours but allow free access to water. If there is any sign of dehydration, dose the dog with Lectade or Electrolyte, which can be obtained from the vet. Both are mixed with water and have immediate

results. A teaspoon of glucose to a teacup of water with a pinch of salt is
another remedy. For mild cases, flat soda water will help and often settles
an upset tummy. A teaspoon of kaogel or kaolin and morphine may be
given at four-hourly intervals. When you start feeding again, give very
small quantities. Arrowroot made up with chicken or rabbit juice is
soothing. Later, a little chicken and rice may be given. Hard-boiled eggs
are very beneficial. If at any time there is any blood in the motion, or the
dog looks in any way distressed, do not hesitate, even if it is the middle of
the night, to call the vet. Diarrhoea can be very weakening, and is often
the prelude to some other nasty disease. Deal with it immediately.

EAR PROBLEMS

If the ears are kept clean and are checked regularly, they cause few
problems; but if they are neglected, they can be a terrible nuisance. For
cleaning, use a little Johnson's Baby Oil warmed and poured in the ear and
then massaged to loosen the wax discharge so that it may be wiped away
with cotton wool buds. If the ears are very inflamed or if you suspect ear
mites, you will need drops from the vet. Once the ears are clean and there
is no inflammation, we use Sherley Canker powder weekly as a
preventative. Remember to treat the cat as well, for they are frequently the
carriers of ear mites.

ECZEMA

Neither King Charles nor Cavaliers are prone to eczema, but occasionally
an extremely sore livid patch can appear as a result of excessive scratching
due to the presence of parasites or dead coat. The vet will probably give an
anti-inflammatory injection and cream to rub into the afflicted area. We
have found Betsolan rubbed in at least four times daily very effective.
Make sure you wash the inflamed area first and remove any particles of
matter with cotton wool and clean boiled water. If it is correctly treated,
the inflammation will clear immediately.

EYE PROBLEMS

If your dog is unlucky enough to hurt his eye, the first thing is to make
sure he does no further damage by rubbing and scratching. Some very
small scratches to the eye can be turned into horrendous self-inflicted
injuries. If you have a number of dogs it is worthwhile investing in one of
the plastic Elizabethan collars from your vet. This can be used in an
emergency and you can travel to the surgery without further damage
ensuing on the journey. You can also convert a plastic colander in an
emergency by cutting a hole in the centre for the dog's head. Minor eye

Tearduct.   *Entropian.*

irritations can be treated with Chloromycetin eye ointment, which can be obtained from your vet. So always keep a tube handy: prompt treatment is so important.

In-growing eyelashes can cause irritation and watering eyes. It is sometimes possible to pluck out the offending lashes, but if they continue to be a source of irritation, your vet will have to operate. Where there is pronounced staining of the face, blocked tear ducts may be the cause. Again, seek veterinary advice. If you notice any anatomical defect of the eye, always consult your vet. Diamondeye used regularly will help with the staining on the face.

Heat Stroke

Prompt action is necessary to bring the temperature down as quickly as possible. Apply pack ice or frozen products round the patient, or cold water. If you are away from home, try to find a stream or any other source of water. After fifteen minutes, allow the dog to rest somewhere cool and quiet. If necessary, take the dog to be checked by your vet. The inside of a car heats up in a very short time during hot weather, so never leave a dog in the car while you are shopping or visiting friends during the summer months. Even if you originally parked in a cool shady place, check the sun has not moved round leaving your dog exposed to the intense heat that builds up so quickly.

Heart Problems

An incessant cough or fainting fits could herald heart problems. When the dog is given its annual booster inoculations, ask your vet to check its heart.

HERNIAS

There are two types of hernia that affect King Charles and Cavaliers. Umbilical hernias are not uncommon: most are very small and seldom cause any trouble but if they harden or enlarge they should be dealt with by surgery immediately. Inguinal hernias, on the other hand, should always be operated on by your vet. When a bitch is in whelp, it is not unknown for a puppy to slip into the groin hernia and for the hernia to strangulate. It should also be remembered there is a very strong school of thought that believes inguinal hernias are hereditary, while many of the umbilical are caused through whelping.

LAMENESS

If a dog suddenly becomes lame, check for the obvious first. If the problem is in the foot the dog will probably hold the offending paw off the ground. If it continues to use the foot, albeit reluctantly, the problem is probably higher up. Check for blisters between the toes, eczema of the feet, sore pads, long and in-growing toe nails, split nails with infection at the nail bed, cuts, thorns penetrating either pads or interdigital spaces, glass or particles of flint penetrating a pad, tar and gravel adhering to the pads, and for sprains. The next stage is to check for bruises and contraction of the tendons, dislocation of the stifle joint and possible fractures.

For blisters between the toes and eczema, bathe the feet in salt water or liquid garlic. With cuts, bathe with Savlon and spray with Terramycin aerosol spray, available from your vet. This can also be used for the eczema and blisters. To remove tar, first cut all the hair from between the pads and soak the foot in vegetable oil. Then rub butter or suntan cream into the paws and wash off with washing-up liquid. If there is an infection in the nail bed, antibiotics from your vet will be necessary. For all dislocations and sprains complete rest will be necessary, but your vet will advise you. Fractures are obviously the vet's province.

PARASITES

Fleas, lice, ticks and harvest mites are the most common parasites found on dogs. With all the washes, powders and sprays available, regular treatment of the dog and carpets and bedding will be all that is necessary. Unless regular treatment is undertaken, re-infestation will occur.

Many King Charles and Cavaliers have sensitive skins which makes them allergic to flea bites, and severe allergic dermatitis can result. Hedgehogs are the biggest flea factory!

POISONS

As with small children, it is better to be safe than sorry and not allow dogs or puppies access to garages and sheds where mechanical oils, paints, garden herbicides and slug pellets are stored. Take care with rat poisons. If you can identify which poison your dog has consumed, take the packet with you to the vet.

Pyometra

Within three weeks of a bitch being in season, check the vulva daily for signs of discharge. In open cases, there is often yellow pus or a red-brown smelly discharge. The bitch often drinks excessively and sometimes vomits. Check immediately with your vet as any delay could cause the death of your bitch. It is not always necessary to remove the uterus as some bitches respond to medical treatment. But we have always found that in the long run the swift removal of the uterus is more successful than treatment, as all appears to lie dormant until the next season when the symptoms reappear with greater ferocity, which then makes an operation essential.

Skin Problems

Skin problems, if neglected for any length of time, can become extremely difficult to eradicate. Parasites, eczema and scurf have already been dealt with. There are two kinds of mange, follicular and sarcoptic. Sarcoptic mange causes frantic scratching and is easily transmissible from one dog to another. Burn all bedding and bathe the dog at regular intervals, in a wash obtainable from your vet, over a period of at least a month. Follicular mange is harder to cure, but must be done under strict veterinary supervision. Follicular mange can be inherited but it is certainly not common in King Charles or Cavaliers. Ringworm is very often overlooked or mistaken for a patch of eczema; only your vet has the ultra-violet equipment to identify the ringworm fungus. The treatment, though tedious, is usually very successful. Constant bathing and a course of pills is necessary.

Snake Bites

Britain's only poisonous snake is the adder, but your dog may be unfortunate enough to become a victim. Act swiftly, keep the dog as calm as possible, and carry him to the vet. If the dog has been bitten on a limb, apply a tourniquet above the bite and release it every fifteen minutes. The venom is at its strongest during the summer months, when the snake is most active. If you suspect you have snakes, eradicate them post haste.

Stings: Wasp and Bee

Both wasps and bees seem to hold a fascination for dogs, who will try and catch them and inevitably get stung. If the sting is visible, pull it out with tweezers, and apply a strong solution of bicarbonate of soda. If the sting is in the mouth or on the lips, apply bicarbonate of soda direct. If there is any danger of the dog having swallowed a bee or wasp, get to your vet immediately. We have found Waspeeze excellent for stings on the feet or body. Another useful remedy is freshly sliced onion rubbed on the affected part, but this is only a temporary measure.

TUMOURS

As dogs get older, small tumours often appear. There are some owners that prefer to leave them alone to take their natural course and only seek surgery when really necessary. The vet is the best person to advise. We feel there is more chance of success if the tumours are removed when small, as this is only a relatively minor operation.

VOMITING

Occasionally dogs vomit up froth, for no apparent reason. Albumen water is an excellent way to settle an irritated stomach. Beat the white of an egg with one rounded teaspoonful of glucose powder and two teaspoons of cold boiled water. If this does not settle the dog's stomach, and vomiting is frequent, veterinary attention is necessary. If vomiting and diarrhoea occur together, consult your vet.

WORMS

Roundworms and tapeworms are the two types of worm the King Charles and Cavalier owner is most likely to deal with. All puppies should be dosed regularly for roundworm. We have found Antepar excellent, as it is entirely safe and may be used from three weeks, if considered necessary. Wormers for adults purchased from your vet are likely to be more effective than those purchased from general shops. Scolaban and Yomesan, the two preparations most effective against tapeworm, can only be purchased from a vet. If a regular worming programme is carried out with adult dogs, no large worm infestations should result.

WOUNDS

Wound powder, available from your vet or sometimes from a good saddlery is excellent for coping with minor cuts and abrasions.

There is a very good chance the only time the vet will see your King Charles or Cavalier is for inoculations and subsequent boosters, as generally both breeds are healthy dogs, requiring little veterinary attention.